Henry Lucas

The Jewish Year

a collection of devotional poems for Sabbaths and holidays throughout the year

Henry Lucas

The Jewish Year
a collection of devotional poems for Sabbaths and holidays throughout the year

ISBN/EAN: 9783337103859

Printed in Europe, USA, Canada, Australia, Japan

Cover: Foto ©Lupo / pixelio.de

More available books at **www.hansebooks.com**

FROM THE LIBRARY OF

REV. LOUIS FITZGERALD BENSON, D. D.

BEQUEATHED BY HIM TO

THE LIBRARY OF

PRINCETON THEOLOGICAL SEMINARY

Division   SCB
Section   14298

THE JEWISH YEAR

THE JEWISH YEAR

A COLLECTION
OF DEVOTIONAL POEMS

FOR

Sabbaths and Holidays throughout the Year

TRANSLATED AND COMPOSED

BY

ALICE LUCAS

London
MACMILLAN AND CO., Limited
NEW YORK   THE MACMILLAN COMPANY
1898

All rights reserved

I DEDICATE THIS BOOK

TO

MY MOTHER

CONTENTS

			PAGE
1. FIRST SABBATH			
Light and Darkness	.	. *Jehuda Halevi* .	1
2. SECOND SABBATH			
God, whom shall I compare to Thee?	. . .	. *Jehuda Halevi* .	3
3. THIRD SABBATH			
Abraham's Faith .		. *Original* .	6
4. FOURTH SABBATH			
The Faithful Men	.	. *Elijah b. Mordecai* .	7
5. FIFTH SABBATH			
A Stranger and a Sojourner am I	. .	. *Original* .	10
6. SIXTH SABBATH			
O Soul, with storms beset	.	*Solomon ibn Gebirol* .	11
7. SEVENTH SABBATH			
Jacob's Dream	. .	. *Original* .	15
8. EIGHTH SABBATH			
Not Worthy .	. .	. *Original* .	17

			PAGE
9.	NINTH SABBATH		
	The Living God	*Abraham ibn Ezra*	19
10.	TENTH SABBATH		
	To the Soul	*Jehuda Halevi*	22
11.	ELEVENTH SABBATH		
	Psalm CXXVI	*Paraphrase*	24
12.	TWELFTH SABBATH		
	The Land of Peace	*Solomon ibn Gebirol*	26
13.	THIRTEENTH SABBATH		
	The Mission of Moses	*A Talmud Legend*	28
14.	FOURTEENTH SABBATH		
	The Sun and Moon	*Jehuda Halevi*	30
15.	FIFTEENTH SABBATH		
	Prayer for Help	*Abraham ibn Ezra*	31
16.	SIXTEENTH SABBATH		
	Lord, do Thou guide me	*Original*	34
17.	SEVENTEENTH SABBATH		
	The Law	*Abraham ibn Ezra*	35
18.	EIGHTEENTH SABBATH		
	Sanctification	*Jehuda ibn Abitur*	37
19.	NINETEENTH SABBATH		
	Offerings	*Original*	42
20.	TWENTIETH SABBATH		
	Even as the Daily Offering	*Solomon ben Abun*	44
21.	TWENTY-FIRST SABBATH		
	Elijah's Prayer	*Jehuda ibn Giat*	46

CONTENTS

22. **TWENTY-SECOND SABBATH**		PAGE
The Sabbath Day.	*Jehuda Halevi* .	51
23. **TWENTY-THIRD SABBATH**		
Hymn of Praise	*Abraham ibn Ezra* .	53
24. **TWENTY-FOURTH SABBATH**		
Guilty are we	*Jehuda Halevi* .	55
25. **TWENTY-FIFTH SABBATH**		
Our Father's Sins.	*From the Portuguese Prayer Book. Author unknown* .	58
26. **TWENTY-SIXTH SABBATH**		
Resignation .	*Abraham ibn Ezra* .	60
27. **TWENTY-SEVENTH SABBATH**		
Simeon Ben Migdal	*A Talmud Legend* .	62
28. **TWENTY-EIGHTH SABBATH**		
Dawn .	*Moses ibn Ezra* .	65
29. **TWENTY-NINTH SABBATH**		
Happy he who saw of old	*Adapted from Solomon ibn Gebirol* .	67
30. **THIRTIETH SABBATH**		
O Sleeper, wake, arise .	*Jehuda Halevi* .	71
31. **THIRTY-FIRST SABBATH**		
At Evening .	*From the Daily Prayer Book. Author unknown*	74
32. **THIRTY-SECOND SABBATH**		
"Praise ye the Almighty"	*From "Tal Orouth." Author unknown* .	76

33. THIRTY-THIRD SABBATH		PAGE
The Wonders of God	*Joab*	78
34. THIRTY-FOURTH SABBATH		
As the Sand of the Sea	*From the Portuguese Prayer Book. Author unknown*	81
35. THIRTY-FIFTH SABBATH		
The Peace of God	*Original*	83
36. THIRTY-SIXTH SABBATH		
Faith	*Original*	84
37. THIRTY-SEVENTH SABBATH		
O thou Red Sea	*Jehuda Halevi*	85
38. THIRTY-EIGHTH SABBATH		
Hillel and his Guest	*A Talmud Legend*	88
39. THIRTY-NINTH SABBATH		
Psalm CXXI	*Paraphrase*	90
40. FORTIETH SABBATH		
The Ways of God	*Jehuda Halevi*	92
41. FORTY-FIRST SABBATH		
The Soul	*Abraham ibn Ezra*	94
42. FORTY-SECOND SABBATH		
Commit thy Way	*Original*	96
43. FORTY-THIRD SABBATH		
Prayer	*Solomon ibn Gebirol*	97
44. FORTY-FOURTH SABBATH		
Yea, more than they	*Original*	98

CONTENTS

45. FORTY-FIFTH SABBATH
    At Morning . . . . *Jehuda Halevi* . . 99

46. FORTY-SIXTH SABBATH
    O Lord, I call on Thee . *Abraham ibn Ezra* . 101

47. FORTY-SEVENTH SABBATH
    Souls of the Righteous . . *Original* . . . 103

48. FORTY-EIGHTH SABBATH
    How Long . . . . *Jehuda Halevi* . . 104

49. FORTY-NINTH SABBATH
    The Commandment of Forgetfulness . . . . *A Talmud Legend* . 105

50. FIFTIETH SABBATH
    From Psalm IV . . . *Original* . . . 107

51. FIFTY-FIRST SABBATH
    Lo, as the Potter . . . *From the Atonement Prayer Book. Author unknown* . 109

52. FIFTY-SECOND SABBATH
    Penitential Prayer . . *Moses ibn Ezra* . 112

53. FIFTY-THIRD SABBATH
    The Death of Moses . . *From the Italian Prayer Book. Author unknown* . 116

54. FIFTY-FOURTH SABBATH
    Hymn of Glory . . . *Jehuda ha Chasid* . 119

55. FIRST DAY OF PASSOVER
    When the Morning came . *Isaac ibn Giat* . . 122

56. **SEVENTH DAY OF PASSOVER**		PAGE
By the Red Sea .	. *Jehuda Halevi* .	125
57. **PENTECOST**		
Sinai . .	. *Jehuda Halevi* .	128
58. **FAST OF AB**		
Ode to Zion .	. *Jehuda Halevi* .	129
59. **NEW YEAR**		
My King .	. *Nachmanides*	134
60. **NEW YEAR**		
Judgment and Mercy .	. *Simeon* . .	137
61. **PENITENTIAL DAYS**		
The Crown of Sovereignty	. *Solomon ibn Gebirol* .	140
DAY OF ATONEMENT		
62. The Heart's Desire .	. *Jehuda Halevi* . .	153
63. Servant of God .	. *Jehuda Halevi* .	156
64. Mercy and Pardon .	. *Chiya* .	159
65. While yet we dwell on earth . . .	. *Author unknown* .	161
66. **FIRST DAY OF TABERNACLES**		
Palms and Myrtles .	. *Kalir* .	163
67. **EIGHTH DAY OF TABERNACLES**		
Creator of the Universe	. *Joseph* . . .	165
68. **SABBATH HYMN** . .	. *Solomon Alkabets*	167
69. **HYMN FOR THE CONCLUSION OF THE SABBATH** .	. *Isaac* .	169

CONTENTS

70. HYMN OF UNITY FOR THE SEVEN DAYS OF THE WEEK	*Samuel bar Kalonymos*	PAGE 171
71. GRACE AFTER MEALS	*Author unknown*	178
72. GRACE FOR SABBATH	*Isaac*	180
73. MORNING AND EVENING HYMNS	*Talmudic. From the Daily Prayer Book*	182
74. LORD OF THE UNIVERSE (ADON OLAM)	*From the Daily Prayer Book. Author unknown*	184
75. THE LIVING GOD WE PRAISE (YIGDAL)	*Daniel b. Judah Dayan*	186

PREFACE

THE present volume has been written to meet, even though inadequately, a long recognised want, namely a collection of hymns and other devotional poems for the use of English Jews. It is composed chiefly of translations from the mediæval Hebrew poets, and includes most of those already published under the title of *Songs of Zion*. The new matter is, however, more than double that of the old, and some original poems, a few paraphrases of Psalms, and three or four versified Talmud legends have also been added. The poems translated are mainly taken from those additions to the Jewish prayer-book which were made after the liturgy had been fixed, so far as its chief features are concerned. Some of these additions are older than the tenth, some are as late as the sixteenth century. They do not appear identically in all forms of the synagogue liturgy, and while some of them readily found a place in the ordinary Sabbath prayers, others enjoyed only a local admission [1] and were used on special occasions only. In the task of discovering poems suitable for translation in the various liturgies and in two or three collections of Hebrew mediæval poetry, in ascertaining the authors of several hymns given anonymously in the prayer-books, and in grappling with many of the difficulties attendant on rendering into English the often involved and obscure Hebrew of the originals, I have received from Mr. Israel Abrahams much valuable aid, which it is a pleasure to me to acknowledge here.

It has not been thought necessary to add either introductory remarks or literary notes to these translations. They are intended for devotional purposes, and it is entirely from this point of view that I have regarded my material. The book is for devotion, not for study. It is meant as an adjunct to the prayer-book, to be used at home, in the Sabbath school, perhaps occasionally in the synagogue,

---

[1] As, *e.g.* the quaint hymn on the death of Moses (see Sabbath 53) which, I believe, is only to be found in the liturgy used by the Italian Jews. It is based on the *Midrash*.

as an aid to religious meditation, derived in a great measure from the prayer-book itself. I have endeavoured to make my translations as accurate as possible; but, though I trust that some of the devotional spirit of the originals has been retained even in an English version, I am regretfully conscious that I have not succeeded in giving them that glow of intense religiousness, which these liturgical poems possess in the Hebrew. Uncouth and laboured as that Hebrew sometimes is, it is never commonplace and never aught but spiritually forcible. It is true the Hebrew mediæval poets wrote for the world as well as for the synagogue. Their works contained satires, love songs, epistles, and epigrams, as well as hymns. But it is beyond question that they were at their best as hymnologists. In devotional poetry they poured forth their whole heart, and their constant theme was the goodness of God and the duty of man. Written in the dark ages of Jewish life, these hymns are illuminated by a divine optimism that may well serve to strengthen our own often wavering faith, and lead us too to find in our religion, that peace and happiness which blessed the singers of those days in the midst of sorrow and persecution.

In the arrangement of the hymns for every Sabbath and festival throughout the year a famous literary precedent has been followed. It must, however, be pointed out that some of the poems here assigned to special Sabbaths are included in some synagogue rituals for every Sabbath. Again, some of the poems here given for Sabbath use were originally composed for more specific occasions, for festivals and fasts. But it must be remembered that very few hymns were written for ordinary Sabbaths, and further that the same hymn will appear in one ritual for an ordinary Sabbath, while in another it will be found appropriated to a special occasion, the truth being that though written for special days, there is seldom anything that renders them inappropriate for all times. Many readers of hymns criticise them as monotonous. Perhaps a similar complaint will be made against this book, especially when it is admitted that hymns written for one day appear equally suitable for another. A further reason for the tendency to monotony in this collection may be found in the fact that hymns of what we may call historic interest, which have reference to such passing events as the founding of a new congregation, or the migration of an old one, the death of a famous Rabbi, or, too often, a more than usually grievous persecution, have been omitted from these pages, as having but little devotional value to the present-day reader. This may somewhat have robbed *The Jewish Year* of the variety which distinguishes the liturgical poetry that responded to every passing phase of life. But the monotony of hymns in general is due to a deeper cause also. There is infinite variety in God's goodness, but man has but a finite faculty for giving expression to it. If there be monotony in the thoughts that animate this and every other collection of hymns, the life of man would nevertheless be the nobler and the better, if it reflected, however faintly, that monotony, that wholehearted faith, that supreme sense of God's love. This is the constant theme of hymns such as are here presented by one who is fully conscious of defects for which she alone is responsible, but who ventures to hope, that a theme so congenial to the highest and noblest ideal of Judaism may yet make these poems acceptable to those for whom they were written.

Sabbath—I

And God said, Let there be light : and there was light.—GENESIS i. 3.

Surely goodness and mercy shall follow me all the days of my life : and I will dwell in the house of the Lord for ever.—PSALM xxiii. 6.

LIGHT AND DARKNESS

O SILENT heart, pour forth thy prayer!
From Meshech's tents of strife and care,
Look up to God, thy rock divine,
Banner and host and refuge thine.
'Tis He who makes thy sun to shine,
Who formeth light and darkness.

His mandate made the earth appear,
And curved the heaven's celestial sphere.
That all might then His glory see,
Nor aught in vain created be,

He called the sun in majesty
To rise and banish darkness.

"Let there be light!" the heavens heard,
And all their host, His mighty word.
Then knew they that a rock of might
Upheld the heaven's highest height,
And praised their Maker for the light
Which overcame the darkness.

Thus will He turn my night to day,
And when I fall, my footsteps stay.
He will my people's light restore,
And make them glad as heretofore.
He is my light for evermore,
Although I sit in darkness.

Sabbath—II

For this is as the waters of Noah unto me: for as I have sworn that the waters of Noah should no more go over the earth; so have I sworn that I would not be wroth with thee, nor rebuke thee. For the mountains shall depart, and the hills be removed; but my kindness shall not depart from thee, neither shall the covenant of my peace be removed, saith the Lord that hath mercy on thee.—ISAIAH liv. 9, 10.

GOD, WHOM SHALL I COMPARE TO THEE?

GOD, whom shall I compare to Thee,
When Thou to none canst likened be?
Under what image shall I dare
To picture Thee, when everywhere
All Nature's forms Thine impress bear?

Greater, O Lord, Thy glories are
Than all the heavenly chariot far.
Whose mind can grasp Thy world's design?

Whose word can fitly Thee define?
Whose tongue set forth Thy powers divine?

Can heart approach, can eye behold
Thee in Thy righteousness untold?
Whom did'st Thou to Thy counsel call,
When there was none to speak withal
Since Thou wast first and Lord of all?

Thy world eternal witness bears
That none its Maker's glory shares.
Thy wisdom is made manifest
In all things formed by Thy behest,
All with Thy seal's clear mark impress'd.

Before the pillars of the sky
Were raised, before the mountains high
Were wrought, ere hills and dales were known,
Thou in Thy majesty alone
Did'st sit, O God, upon Thy throne!

Hearts, seeking Thee, from search refrain,
And weary tongues their praise restrain.
Thyself unbound by time and place,
Thou dost pervade, support, embrace
The world and all created space.

The sages' minds bewildered grow,
The lightning speed of thought is slow.
"Awful in praises" art Thou named;
Thou fillest, strong in strength proclaimed,
This universe Thy hand has framed.

Deep, deep beyond all fathoming,
Far, far beyond all measuring,
We can but seek Thy deeds alone;
When bow Thy saints before Thy throne
Then is Thy faithfulness made known.

Thy righteousness we can discern,
Thy holy law proclaim and learn.
Is not Thy presence near alway
To them who penitently pray,
But far from those who sinning stray?

Pure souls behold Thee, and no need
Have they of light: they hear and heed
Thee with the mind's keen ear, although
The ear of flesh be dull and slow.
Their voices answer to and fro.

Thy holiness for ever they proclaim:
The Lord of Hosts! thrice holy is His name!

Sabbath—III

After these things the word of the Lord came unto Abram in a vision, saying, Fear not, Abram : I am thy shield, and thy exceeding great reward. . . . And he believed in the Lord; and he counted it to him for righteousness.—GENESIS xv. 1 and 6.

ABRAHAM'S FAITH

AND the Lord said : "Look now towards heaven and
    see
If thou can'st number there the numberless
Great host of stars—even thus thy seed shall be,"
And Abraham believed in God, and He
Counted it unto him for righteousness.
Happy art thou, who through life's storm and stress
Dost hold thy faith in God unceasingly,
His mercy will not leave thee comfortless,
But with exceeding peace thy soul will bless,
Yea, and thy faith shall be accounted thee
                     For righteousness.

Sabbath—IV

What prayer or what supplication soever shall be made of any man, or of all thy people Israel, when every one shall know his own sore and his own grief, and shall spread forth his hands in this house: then hear thou from heaven thy dwelling-place, and forgive, and render unto every man according unto all his ways, whose heart thou knowest; (for thou only knowest the hearts of the children of men).—2 CHRONICLES vi. 29, 30.

Thou wilt perform the truth to Jacob, and the mercy to Abraham, which thou hast sworn unto our fathers from the days of old.—MICAH vii. 20.

THE FAITHFUL MEN

THE faithful men have perished one by one,
And there remaineth none
To stand, with words entreating thee—
Even as Abraham with his prayer,
Saying—"Yet lacking still may be
Five of the fifty righteous there."
And God made answer then:
"Yea, I will spare the city even for ten!"

The faithful men have perished one by one,
And there remaineth none,
Holy and strong Thy grace to win
Even as Amram's son did pray;
"Lord, if Thou pardon not their sin
Blot me from out Thy book this day."
And answer made the Lord:
"Pardoned have I, according to thy word."

The faithful men have perished one by one,
And there remaineth none
Help in the perilous hour to bring,
Even as Aaron swiftly ran
Forth with his incense-offering,
When that the pestilence began.
The living and the dead
Between he stood and lo! the plague was stayed.

The faithful men have perished one by one,
And there remaineth none
Thy mercy fitly to implore,
As David did, when, sore distress'd
Beside Araunah's threshing floor
He twice declared: I have transgress'd.
Thus prayed he penitent,
And the Almighty ceased from chastisement.

THE FAITHFUL MEN

The faithful men have perished one by one,
And there remaineth none
To trust Thee with a perfect heart,
Like to Elijah, when he stood,
Praying in Carmel's mount, apart,
And poured the water on the wood.
And lo! God's answer came,
Even at the Mincha hour in heavenly flame.

The faithful men have perished one by one,
And there remaineth none
With ceaseless prayer to seek thine aid,
Pleading for pardon, even as he
The faithful of Thy house, who prayed
By day and night incessantly.
Yet as in days of old
Have mercy on us, Lord, with mercies manifold.

Sabbath—V

Hear my prayer, O Lord, and give ear unto my cry; hold not thy peace at my tears: for I am a stranger with thee, and a sojourner, as all my fathers were.—Psalm xxxix. 12.

A STRANGER AND A SOJOURNER AM I

A stranger and a sojourner am I
With Thee, O Lord, who hast on me bestowed
For a brief space, a pilgrim's scant abode,
A little field and toilsome husbandry.

A stranger and a sojourner! I sigh,
And fain had rested, when the noon-day glowed,
Neath the cool shade, where crystal waters flowed,
But time speeds on apace, the hours fly.

A stranger! yea, but Thou, O Lord, art nigh;
A sojourner! yea, but the weary load
I bear, Thy hand that traced the wanderer's road
Shall ease me of, beneath the sunset sky.

Sabbath—VI

Thou shalt guide me with thy counsel, and afterward receive me to glory. Whom have I in heaven but thee? and there is none upon earth that I desire beside thee. My flesh and my heart faileth: but God is the strength of my heart, and my portion for ever.—PSALM lxxiii. 24-26.

O SOUL, WITH STORMS BESET!

O SOUL, with storms beset,
Thy griefs and cares forget!
Why dread earth's transient woe,
When soon thy body in the grave unseen
    Shall be laid low,
And all will be forgotten then, as though
    It had not been?

Wherefore, my soul, be still!
Adore God's holy will,
Fear death's supreme decree.

Thus mayst thou save thyself, and win high aid
    To profit thee,
When thou, returning to thy Lord, shalt see
    Thy deeds repaid.

Why muse, O troubled soul,
    O'er life's poor earthly goal?
    When thou hast fled, the clay
Lies mute, nor bear'st thou aught of wealth, or might
    With thee that day,
But, like a bird, unto thy nest away,
    Thou wilt take flight.

Why for a land lament
    In which a lifetime spent
    Is as a hurried breath?
Where splendour turns to gloom, and honours show
    A faded wreath,
Where health and healing soon must sink beneath
    The fatal bow.

What seemeth good and fair
    Is often falsehood there.
    Gold melts like shifting sands,
Thy hoarded riches pass to other men,
    And strangers' hands,

And what will all thy treasured wealth and lands
   Avail thee then?

Life is a vine, whose crown
   The reaper Death cuts down.
   His ever-watchful eyes
Mark every step, until night's shadows fall,
   And swiftly flies
The passing day, and ah! how distant lies
   The goal of all.

Therefore, rebellious soul,
   Thy base desires control;
   With scantly given bread
Content thyself, nor let thy memory stray
   To splendours fled,
But call to mind affliction's weight, and dread
   The judgment day.

Prostrate and humbled go,
   Like to the dove laid low,
   Remember evermore
The peace of heaven, the Lord's eternal rest.
   When burdened sore
With sorrow's load, at every step implore
   His succour bless'd.

>   Before God's mercy-seat
>   His pardoning love entreat.
>   Make pure thy thoughts from sin,
> And bring a contrite heart as sacrifice
>   His grace to win—
> Then will His angels come and lead thee in
>   To Paradise.

Sabbath—VII

Surely the Lord is in this place ; and I knew it not . . . .
this is none other but the house of God, and this is the gate of
heaven.—GENESIS xxviii. 16, 17.

Cast thy burden upon the Lord, and he shall sustain thee : he
shall never suffer the righteous to be moved.—PSALM lv. 22.

JACOB'S DREAM

"THIS is no other than the house of God,"
He said, "and this the gate of heaven."
He who all day the path to Haran trod,
    And came to Luz at even.

He who in dreams beheld a vision there—
A ladder reaching to the sky,
Whereon ascending and descending were
    God's angels ceaselessly.

And when he saw Him standing at the head
Proclaiming Israel's chosen lot,

"Surely the Lord is in this place" he said,
  "Although I knew it not.

"How awful is this place!" And ere he went
His way he raised an altar there,
And offered to the Lord Omnipotent
  The sacrifice of prayer.

And Beth-El did they call that place, the name
Of which was Luz in days of yore,
The house of God—thus in a word to frame
  That vision evermore.

O golden dream of faith's primeval days!
Symbol to later ages given,
Telling that God is everywhere always,
  And earth the gate to heaven.

Sabbath—VIII

I am not worthy of the least of all the mercies, and of all the truth, which thou hast shewed unto thy servant; for with my staff I passed over this Jordan; and now I am become two bands.—GENESIS xxxii. 10.

Commit thy way unto the Lord.—PSALM xxxvii. 5.

NOT WORTHY

I AM not worthy of the least of all
The mercies and the truth which thou hast shewed
Unto Thy servant, for this road
I traversed and this Jordan cross'd
With but my staff for aid and load,
And now I am become a twofold host.

I am not worthy, Lord, I cry this day,
Not worthy of the gracious heavenly care
With which Thou guidest everywhere
Thy children, though the path may be

Narrow or stony, steep or bare,
That leads at last earth's pilgrim home to thee.

I am not worthy of Thy holy word,
That bids us unto Thee commit our ways,
And move, illumined by the rays
Of steadfast faith's eternal light,
Unharmed through life's oft darkened days,
Until we come where there is no more night.

I am not worthy—yea, but greater far
Is Thy great love than my unworthiness,
Thy love, that cannot pitiless
Our sorrows and our sins behold,
That comes to pardon and to bless,
And gives us peace as in the days of old.

Sabbath—IX

Ye shall do my judgments, and keep mine ordinances, to walk therein : I am the Lord your God. Ye shall therefore keep my statutes, and my judgments : which if a man do, he shall live in them.—LEVITICUS xviii. 4, 5.

Thou openest thine hand, and satisfiest the desire of every living thing. . . . My mouth shall speak the praise of the Lord : and let all flesh bless his holy name for ever and ever.—PSALM cxlv. 16 and 21.

THE LIVING GOD

ATHIRST for God, to Him my soul aspires,
The living God it is my heart desires.

The living God created me
To life. Yea, as I live, spake He,
No living man my face shall see,
Shall see my face and live.

He fashioned all with counsel wise
And purpose wonderful that lies

For ever hidden from our eyes,
The eyes of all who live.

Supreme o'er all His glory reigns,
Extolled on earth in holy strains,
Blessed is he whose hand maintains
The soul of all who live.

He separated Israel's seed,
To teach them statutes, which indeed
If that a man do hear and heed,
His soul by them shall live.

Can pure and just themselves declare
They who of dust created were?
Lo, in Thy sight, O Lord, we dare
Call no man just who lives.

Like serpent's poison venomous,
The sinful passion dwells in us,
Can then from evil cankerous
Be any free that live?

But they the cords of sin who break
May yet the evil path forsake,
Ere in that house their rest they take,
That waits for all who live.

THE LIVING GOD

Call us in mercy unto Thee
Again Thy witnesses to be,
O Thou, who openest graciously
Thy hand to all that live.

Low to the earth my head I bow,
With hands outspread, repeating now,
"Blessed, O Lord our God, be Thou
By every soul that lives!"

Sabbath—X

Gracious is the Lord, and righteous; yea, our God is merciful. The Lord preserveth the simple: I was brought low, and he helped me. Return unto thy rest, O my soul; for the Lord hath dealt bountifully with thee.—PSALM cxvi. 5-7.

Arise ye, and depart; for this is not your rest.—MICAH ii. 10.

TO THE SOUL

O THOU, who springest gloriously
From thy Creator's fountain bless'd!
Arise, depart, for this is not thy rest.
The way is long, thou must preparéd be,
Thy Maker bids thee seek thy goal—
Return then to thy rest, my soul,
For bountifully has God dealt with thee.

Behold I am a stranger here,
My days like fleeting shadows seem.
When wilt thou, if not now, thy life redeem?

And when thou seek'st thy Maker have no fear,
For if thou have but purified
Thy heart from stain of sin and pride,
Thy righteous deeds to him shall draw thee near.

O thou in strength who treadest, learn
To know thyself, cast dreams away!
The goal is distant far, and short the day.
What can'st thou plead th' Almighty's grace to earn?
Wouldst thou the glory of the Lord
Behold, O soul? With prompt accord
Then to thy father's house, return, return!

Sabbath—XI

They that sow in tears shall reap in joy. He that goeth forth and weepeth, bearing precious seed, shall doubtless come again with rejoicing, bringing his sheaves with him.—Psalm cxxvi. 5 and 6.

PARAPHRASE OF PSALM CXXVI

When that the Lord did turn again
Of Zion the captivity,
Like unto them that dream were we
Then were our hearts with gladness thrilled
Then was our mouth with laughter filled,
    And songs unceasingly.

The heathen said, The Lord hath done
For them great things and glorious.
The Lord hath done great things for us.
Turn our captivity again,
O Lord, as in the southern plain,
    The streams do gladden us.

Who sows in tears shall reap in joy;
And he who goeth forth in need,
Weeping and bearing precious seed,
Shall doubtless, all his toil o'erpast,
Unto his home return at last
    Bringing his sheaves indeed.

Sabbath—XII

Thou wilt shew me the path of life: in thy presence is fulness of joy; at thy right hand there are pleasures for evermore.—PSALM xvi. 11.

THE LAND OF PEACE

WHOSE works, O Lord, like Thine can be,
   Who 'neath Thy throne of grace,
For those pure souls from earth set free,
   Hast made a dwelling-place?

There are the sinless spirits bound
   Up in the bond of life,
The weary there new strength have found,
   The weak have rest from strife.

Sweet peace and calm their spirits bless,
   Who reach that heavenly home,

And never-ending pleasantness—
Such is the world to come.

There glorious visions manifold
    Those happy ones delight,
And in God's presence they behold
    Themselves and Him aright.

In the King's palace they abide,
    And at His table eat,
With kingly dainties satisfied,
    Spiritual food most sweet.

This is the rest for ever sure,
    This is the heritage,
Whose goodness and whose bliss endure
    Unchanged from age to age.

This is the land the spirit knows,
    That everlastingly
With milk and honey overflows—
    And such its fruit shall be.

Sabbath—XIII

Thou shalt love thy neighbour as thyself : I am the Lord.—Leviticus xix. 18.

The king that faithfully judgeth the poor, his throne shall be established for ever.—Proverbs xxix. 14.

THE MISSION OF MOSES

While Israel in Egypt toiled and wept
Moses afar the sheep of Jethro kept,
Unconscious of the coming word of God,
Following his flocks, the desert path he trod,
And as he sought to gather them one day,
A half-grown lamb chanced from the fold to stray.

He called the wand'rer back, but all in vain
And far he followed it across the plain,
Until at last, beside a streamlet's brink,
He saw the wearied creature stop to drink.

"Yea," Moses said, "in sooth I did not guess
'Twas thirst that made thee my command transgress.

"Thou hast come far—perchance art wearied sore."
And homeward in his arms the lamb he bore.
Then spoke the Lord, "Since thus thy love provides
For these poor sheep that man to thee confides,
As thy soul liveth I will trust to thee
My flock—my people's shepherd thou shalt be."

Sabbath—XIV

The heavens declare the glory of God; and the firmament sheweth his handywork.—PSALM xix. 1.

And it shall be said in that day, Lo, this is our God; we have waited for him, and he will save us: this is the Lord; we have waited for him, we will be glad and rejoice in his salvation.—ISAIAH xxv. 9.

THE SUN AND MOON FOR EVER SHINE

THE sun and moon for ever shine—By day
And night they mark the Eternal's high design,
Changeless and tireless, speeding on their way,
    The sun and moon for ever shine.

Symbols are they of Israel's chosen line,
A nation still though all around decay,
A nation still though countless foes combine,
Smitten by God and healed by God are they.
They shall not fear, safe 'neath the Rock divine
Nor cease to be, until men cease to say,
    The sun and moon for ever shine.

Sabbath—XV

Fear thou not; for I am with thee: be not dismayed; for I am thy God: I will strengthen thee; yea, I will help thee; yea, I will uphold thee with the right hand of my righteousness.
—Isaiah xli. 10.

PRAYER FOR HELP

Lord, I pray with hands uplifted
And my tears flow fast,
For my manifold transgressions
And my sinful past.
Heal mine inward wound and straighten
All my ways at last.
Merciful, O Father, be,
Even when Thou judgest me,
Answer when I call on Thee,
God of my salvation!

Glad yet fearful, I am seeking
Pardon, 'midst the throng

Of Thy chosen congregation
With sweet sound of song,
Hymns and praise and patient striving
To amend the wrong.
Lord, Thy power I will proclaim,
And exalt Thy glorious name,
Yea, my love for Thee like flame
Burns, Thou my salvation!

Thou o'er heavenly heights who ridest
Know'st the inmost parts,
And Thy love accepts repentance
When it sorest smarts,
Counting it as off'rings, ever
Strengthening feeble hearts.
Thou wilt lead Thy flock aright
To the land of my delight,
Thou my refuge, rock, and might,
Heritage and portion.

Well-spring Thou of strength and gladness,
Lord, I hope in Thee,
And declare the power eternal
Of Thy sovereignty.
O! command Thou Thy salvation
To abide with me.
Let it guide me on my way,

Evermore my help and stay,
Bringing me from day to day
Still my daily portion.

Thou wilt save me, Thou wilt guard me,
Mine exalted King.
Have regard to my entreaty
And good tidings bring.
Unto us Thy needy people
Let Thine answer ring:
Fear thou not, for I behold thee,
I will strengthen and enfold thee,
Yea, my right hand shall uphold thee!
I am thy salvation!

Sabbath—XVI

When thou passest through the waters, I will be with thee; and through the rivers, they shall not overflow thee: when thou walkest through the fire, thou shalt not be burned; neither shall the flame kindle upon thee.—Isaiah xliii. 2.

LORD, DO THOU GUIDE ME

Lord, do Thou guide me on my pilgrim way,
Then shall I be at peace, whate'er betide me;
The morn is dark, the clouds hang low and grey,
   Lord, do Thou guide me.

Let not the mists of sin from Thee divide me,
But pierce their gloom with mercy's golden ray,
Then shall I know that Thou in love hast tried me.

O'er rugged paths be Thou my staff and stay,
Beneath thy wings from storm and tempest hide me,
Through life to death, through death to heavenly day—
   Lord, do Thou guide me!

Sabbath—XVII

And Moses came and called for the elders of the people, and laid before their faces all these words which the Lord commanded him. And all the people answered together, and said, All that the Lord hath spoken we will do.—EXODUS xix. 7, 8.

The law of the Lord is perfect, converting the soul; the testimony of the Lord is sure, making wise the simple.—PSALM xix. 7.

THE LAW

My help, my hope, my strength shall be,
Thou perfect law of God, in thee!

My faith shall be my rock of might,
Its law my portion and my right,
Its testimonies my delight,
And day by day, my voice I raise
In song and hymn to chant their praise.

How did th' angelic hosts lament
When from their midst, by God's intent,

The holy law to earth was sent.
"Woe that the pure and sanctified
Should now on sinful lips abide."

The people trembled when they saw
Approaching them the heavenly law—
Their voices rose in joy and awe:
" Thy covenant, O Lord, fulfil,
Declare it, we will do Thy will."

Great wonders He on Sinai wrought,
When unto us His law He taught,
Wherefore to praise His name I sought;
But what am I and what my words
Before the Almighty Lord of lords?

Hear Thou Thy people's prayer, O King,
When like the heavenly host they sing
Thrice Holy, Holy—uttering
Sweet hymns and songs of pleasantness
With joy and awe Thy name to bless.

Sabbath—XVIII

And one cried unto another, and said, Holy, holy, holy, is the Lord of hosts; the whole earth is full of his glory.—ISAIAH vi. 3.

One thing have I desired of the Lord, that will I seek after; that I may dwell in the house of the Lord all the days of my life, to behold the beauty of the Lord, and to enquire in his temple.—PSALM xxvii. 4.

SANCTIFICATION

THE sixfold winged angels cry
To Him who hates iniquity:
  Holy art thou, O Lord,
  Holy art thou!

The mighty ones of earth do call
To Him, who has created all:
  Blessed art Thou, O Lord,
  Blessed art Thou!

They, who in radiance shine, proclaim
Of Him who wrought them out of flame :
    Holy art Thou, O Lord,
      Holy art Thou !

Those doubly tried by flood and fire
United chant in frequent choir :
    Blessed art Thou, O Lord,
      Holy and bless'd !

Pure spheres celestial echoing round
With voice of sweetest song resound :
    Holy art Thou, O Lord,
      Holy art Thou !

All those redeeméd, not by gold,
Repeat in faith and joy untold :
    Blessed art Thou, O Lord,
      Blessed art Thou !

They who pass swiftly to and fro
Make answer as they come and go :
    Holy art Thou, O Lord,
      Holy art Thou !

Who seek His law and testify
That there is none besides Him, cry :

SANCTIFICATION

    Blessed art Thou, O Lord,
    Holy and bless'd!

The hosts of radiant seraphs call
To Him, most glorious of them all:
    Holy art Thou, O Lord,
    Holy art Thou!

The sons of mighty men declare
His majesty beyond compare:
    Blessed art Thou, O Lord,
    Blessed art Thou!

All they who glorify His name
With every morn anew proclaim:
    Holy art Thou, O Lord,
    Holy art Thou!

Israel, His people, ceaselessly
Cry as they bend and bow the knee:
    Blessed art Thou, O Lord,
    Holy and bless'd!

Those shining as a crystal spring,
Chant in the presence of their king:
    Holy art Thou, O Lord,
    Holy art Thou!

The stranger's children evermore
The mighty Lord of lords adore:
   Blessed art Thou, O Lord,
     Blessed art Thou!

Those who of fire are fashioned, crowd
On crowd unnumbered, chant aloud:
   Holy art Thou, O Lord,
     Holy art Thou!

They cry, whom He has freed from thrall,
And His inheritance does call:
   Blessed art Thou, O Lord,
     Holy and bless'd!

Pure visions, bathed in endless light,
Declare 'midst radiance infinite:
   Holy art Thou, O Lord,
     Holy art Thou!

Who to the covenant adhere,
The remnant saved, cry loud and clear:
   Blessed art Thou, O Lord,
     Blessed art Thou!

'Neath folded wings, in cadence meet,
The glorious ones each hour repeat:

SANCTIFICATION

Holy art Thou, O Lord,
Holy art Thou!

She, who among the nations dwells
Chosen, apart, His glory tells :
Holy art Thou, O Lord,
Holy and bless'd!

The high exalted ones make known
Of Him, who fills the heavenly throne :
Holy art Thou, O Lord,
Holy art Thou!

They who their God each day proclaim
"Awful in deeds," exalt His name :
Blessed art Thou, O Lord,
Blessed art Thou!

Those who are awe-inspiring say
Of Him more awful far than they :
Holy art Thou, O Lord,
Holy art Thou!

To all creation's King of kings
From earth, from heaven, responsive rings :
Holy art Thou, O Lord,
Holy and bless'd!

Sabbath—XIX

And the Lord spake unto Moses, saying, Speak unto the children of Israel, that they bring me an offering : of every man that giveth it willingly with his heart ye shall take my offering.—Exodus xxv. 1, 2.

And king David said to Ornan . . . I will not take that which is thine for the Lord, nor offer burnt offerings without cost.—1 Chronicles xxi. 24.

OFFERINGS

Shall I offer unto the Lord
That which has cost me naught,
That which I have not bought
For silver and gold at a price?
Shall I to God's altar bring
Thine oxen for offering?
Then thine, not mine, were the sacrifice.

Let me not bring thee, O Lord,
That which has cost me nought,
Prayers that I have not sought

To shape to my spirit's need,
Resolves half-hearted and faint,
And hopes and longings that paint
Joys of earth's giving, not heavenly meed.

Lord, let me bring unto Thee
Prayers that true faith has wrought,
Self-sacrifice, dearly bought,
And patience, whose lamp never dies,
With penitence, set apart;
For a broken and contrite heart
O Lord, Thou wilt not despise.

𝔖𝔞𝔟𝔟𝔞𝔱𝔥—XX

Wherewith shall I come before the Lord, and bow myself before the high God? shall I come before him with burnt offerings, with calves of a year old? . . . He hath shewed thee, O man, what is good; and what doth the Lord require of thee, but to do justly, and to love mercy, and to walk humbly with thy God?—MICAH vi. 6 and 8.

EVEN AS THE DAILY OFFERING

JUDGE of the earth, who wilt arraign
The nations at Thy judgment seat,
With life and favour bless again
Thy people prostrate at Thy feet.
And mayest Thou our morning prayer
Receive, O Lord, as though it were
The offering that was wont to be
Brought day by day continually.

Thou who art clothed with righteousness,
Supreme, exalted over all—

How oft soever we transgress
Do Thou with pardoning love recall
Those who in Hebron sleep: and let
Their memory live before Thee yet,
Even as the offering unto Thee
Offered of old continually.

Trust in God's strength and be ye strong,
My people, and His laws obey,
Then will He pardon sin and wrong,
Then mercy will His wrath outweigh.
Seek ye His presence and implore
His countenance for evermore,
Then shall your prayers accepted be
As offerings brought continually.

Sabbath—XXI

And Elijah said, How long halt ye between two opinions? if the Lord be God, follow him: but if Baal, then follow him. —1 KINGS xviii. 21.

Yet I have left me seven thousand in Israel, all the knees which have not bowed unto Baal, and every mouth which hath not kissed him.—1 KINGS xix. 18.

ELIJAH'S PRAYER

THE glory of the Lord I will declare
At eventide, when rose Elijah's prayer,
What time, the weak and sinful multitude
From day to day their evil works pursued,
And those who feared the Lord were sore distress'd,
Brought low, and by their enemies oppress'd.
Then while the people gazed, the priests of sin
Were gathered unto him, who sought to win
The erring crowd to hear his holy word,
Acceptable and pleasing to the Lord.

"Oh may my prayer approach Thy throne, Most High,
And be Thine ear attentive to my cry,
When that the hour of Mincha draweth nigh."

Thus, unto all the people clust'ring round,
His words of gracious wisdom did resound,
Each unto each with understanding bound.

"Oh foolish and unwise, who nothing know,
How long, unsure and halting, will ye go,
'Twixt two opinions, ever to and fro?

"Seek where the truth is found—if in the Lord
Or in another—be the truth adored."
And all the people answered not a word.

He cried aloud: "Nay, hearken once again.
I, only I, of all the many slain
A prophet of the Lord alone remain.

"The while the priests of Baal, who daily stand
Bending before the works of craftsmen's hand,
Four hundred count and fifty in the land.

"Choose ye a bullock then with fitting care,
And offer it upon your altar there.
I for myself will likewise mine prepare.

"Then this to all who fain the truth would see,
And follow after it a sign shall be—
Who answereth with fire, God is he."

And they, when these wise words to silence fell,
Seemed to repent, whose hearts did erst rebel,
For all made answer: It is spoken well!

"Be ye, the many, first," he said again,
"Prepare your altar, bring the bullock slain,
But let the fire unkindled yet remain."

They called in folly on an empty name,
"O Baal, answer us, thy power proclaim!"
But neither voice, nor sound for answer came.

Then mocked Elijah them and mocking said:
"Call with a loud voice, be ye not afraid,
Call, for he is a god—be undismayed."

Then leaped they on the altar they had built,
And cut and gashed themselves with knives, and spilt
Their blood with evil rites of shame and guilt.

Weary they grew and faint, as time sped by,
And their souls sank within them hopelessly,
Until the hour of Mincha had come nigh.

The man of God, the prophet, then ignored
For a brief period the holy word,[1]
While he repaired the altar of the Lord.

For every tribe, as was their wont always,
He took a stone, as in the ancient days,
Wherewith the altar of the Lord to raise.

He laid the offering, duly purified,
Upon the altar, and on every side
He dug a trench around it, deep and wide.

"Fill it with water till it overflows,"
He bade them next. Then at the long day's close,
Even at the Mincha hour, Elijah's prayer arose.

   O Lord of all!
God of my fathers, hear me when I call.
   Let it be known
For evermore that Thou art Lord alone;
   That I, even I,
Thy servant am, who still unceasingly
   To serve Thee run,
And at Thy bidding all these things have done.
   Hear, when I pray,
And make Thy people know Thy power this day,

---

[1] The commandment to build an altar in Jerusalem only.

And turn once more
Their hearts to Thee, as in the days of yore

Then fell there fire from heaven at his word,
And all the people cried with one accord,
"The Lord is God—He only—God and Lord!"

Sabbath—XXII

Six days shall work be done, but on the seventh day there shall be to you an holy day, a sabbath of rest to the Lord.—EXODUS xxxv. 2.

If thou turn away thy foot from the sabbath, from doing thy pleasure on my holy day; and call the sabbath a delight, the holy of the Lord, honourable; and shalt honour him, not doing thine own ways, nor finding thine own pleasure, nor speaking thine own words: then shalt thou delight thyself in the Lord; and I will cause thee to ride upon the high places of the earth, and feed thee with the heritage of Jacob thy father: for the mouth of the Lord hath spoken it.—ISAIAH lviii. 13, 14.

THE SABBATH DAY

I

The morning stars chant forth their hymn of praise
For with the light Thou givest them they shine
And at their posts God's angels stand always,
To glorify the holy name divine.
And even so on earth Thy children gather
Within Thy house, to seek their heavenly Father.

Sabbath—XXIII

My times are in thy hand.—PSALM xxxi. 15.

The Lord redeemeth the soul of his servants : and none of them that trust in him shall be desolate.—PSALM xxxiv. 22.

HYMN OF PRAISE

O GOD of earth and heaven,
Spirit and flesh are Thine!
Thou hast in wisdom given,
Man's inward light divine ;
And unto him Thy grace accords
The gift of spoken words.
The world was fashioned by Thy will,
Nor did'st Thou toil at it, for still
Thy breath did Thy design fulfil.

My times are in Thy hand,
Thou knowest what is best,

And where I fear to stand,
Thy strength brings succour bless'd.
Thy loving-kindness, as within
A mantle, hides my sin.
Thy mercies are my sure defence,
And for Thy bounteous providence
Thou dost demand no recompense.

For all the sons of men
Thou hast a book prepared
Where, without hand or pen,
Their deeds are all declared:
Yet for the pure in heart shall be
A pardon found with Thee.
The life and soul Thou did'st create
Thou hast redeemed from evil strait,
Thou hast not left me desolate.

The heavens Thou badest be,
Thy bright, celestial throne,
Are witnesses to Thee,
O Thou the Lord alone.
One, indivisible, Thy name
Upholds creation's frame.
Thou madest all—the depth, the height,
Thou rulest all in power and might,
Supreme, eternal, infinite!

Sabbath—XXIV

Remember not the sins of my youth, nor my transgressions: according to thy mercy remember thou me for thy goodness' sake, O Lord.—PSALM xxv. 7.

I have blotted out, as a thick cloud, thy transgressions, and, as a cloud, thy sins: return unto me; for I have redeemed thee.—ISAIAH xliv. 22.

GUILTY ARE WE

EVIL seed our sins have sown,
Evil fruit from them has grown,
Seek we then, to end our woes,
Him who knows our frame and knows
    That dust are we.

Smitten are we and contrite.
Lo! the heavens in His sight
Are not pure, nor angel band
Stainless: how before Him stand
    Then can we?

Earth-born creatures, wrought of clay,
Dare we boast us of to-day,
When to-morrow, ended all,
To the land beyond recall
    Journey we.

Froward folly led us wrong,
Our deliverance tarries long.
For the harvest moon is set
And the summer past, nor yet
    Saved are we.

Chastised long our fathers were—
Shall we still the burden bear
Of their sins? Nay, grant, Most High,
Us to live and not to die,
    Even we.

Unto God our souls we trust,
Though our bodies sink to dust.
Rich and poor, the self-same seed,
All one's father's sons indeed
    Are not we?

Ye unto His word who cling
Know that God is Lord and King,

Ruling all. The eternal Rock,
He the Shepherd, we the flock,
   His are we.

Vain the wisdom is of man,
He who knoweth not his span,
Nor the hour of life's decay,
We are but of yesterday,
   Naught know we.

Hearken to Thy servant's prayer,
For our souls are filled with care,
Courage fails and hope grows less,
Exiled and in great distress
   Now are we.

Comfort from Thy word we take
That Thou, for Thy mercy's sake,
Wilt avert Thy chastisement
From the truly penitent :
   Wherefore we
Do declare that verily,
   Guilty are we.

Sabbath—XXV

. . . It is of the Lord's mercies that we are not consumed, because his compassions fail not. They are new every morning : great is thy faithfulness. The Lord is my portion, saith my soul: therefore will I hope in him.—LAMENTATIONS iii. 22-24.

Take with you words, and turn to the Lord : say unto him, Take away all iniquity, and receive us graciously : so will we render the calves of our lips.—HOSEA xiv. 2.

OUR FATHERS' SINS

OUR fathers' sins wrought Zion's swift decay,
Priest, altar, sanctuary have passed away.
Yea, words for sacrifice we bring to-day,
And with our lips the steers we will repay.

Destroyed our dwelling lies,
Wasted our house of glorious memories,
The clouds of incense fail,
Gone is our altar, rent the golden veil,
Nought but our prayers remain—

Forgive then our transgressions once again,
As when the appointed one
Led forth the scapegoat to the desert lone.
Have mercy, Lord, and hear us when we pray,
And with our lips the steers we will repay.

The humble and oppress'd
Forgive, O Lord, with mercy ever bless'd,
And let their prayerful cry
Ascend to Thee, like incense breathed on high.
Pardon their manifold
Transgressions, as when, in the days of old,
The priest, with hands outspread,
Made his confession o'er the scapegoat's head.
Answer us, Lord, and turn Thy wrath away,
And with our lips the steers we will repay.

Sabbath—XXVI

Look at the generations of old and see; did ever any trust in the Lord and was confounded? or did any abide in his fear and was forsaken? or whom did he ever despise that called upon him?—ECCLESIASTICUS ii. 10.

Light is sown for the righteous, and gladness for the upright in heart.—PSALM xcvii. 11.

RESIGNATION

I HOPE for the salvation of the Lord,
    In Him I trust, when fears my being thrill,
Come life, come death, according to His word,
    He is my portion still.

Hence doubting heart! I will the Lord extol
    With gladness, for in Him is my desire,
Which, as with fatness, satisfies my soul,
    That doth to heaven aspire.

All that is hidden, shall mine eyes behold,
    And the great Lord of all be known to me,
Him will I serve, His am I as of old;
    I ask not to be free.

Sweet is ev'n sorrow coming in His name,
    Nor will I seek its purpose to explore,
His praise will I continually proclaim,
    And bless Him evermore.

Sabbath—XXVII

For thou lovest all the things that are, and abhorrest nothing which thou hast made : for never wouldest thou have made any thing, if thou hadst hated it. But thou sparest all, for they are thine, O Lord, thou lover of souls.—WISDOM OF SOLOMON xi. 24 and 26.

SIMEON BEN MIGDAL

SIMEON ben Migdal, at the close of day
Upon the shores of ocean chanced to stray,
And there a man of form and mien uncouth,
Dwarfed and mis-shapen, met he on the way.

"Hail, Rabbi," spoke the stranger passing by,
But Simeon thus, discourteous, made reply :
"Say, are there in thy city many more,
Like unto thee, an insult to the eye?"

"Nay, that I cannot tell," the wand'rer said,
"But if thou fain would'st ply the scorner's trade,

Go first and ask the Master Potter why
He has a vessel so mis-shapen made."

Then (so the legend tells) the Rabbi knew
That he had sinned, and prone himself he threw
Before the other's feet, and prayed of him
Pardon for words that now his soul did rue.

But still the other answered as before:
"Go, in the Potter's ear thy plaint outpour,
For what am I? His hand has fashioned me,
And I in humble faith that hand adore."

Brethren, do we not often too forget
Whose hand it is that many a time has set
A radiant soul in an unlovely form
A fair white bird caged in a mouldering net?

Nay, more, do not life's times and chances, sent
By the great Artificer with intent
That they should prove a blessing, oft appear
To us a burden that we sore lament.

Ah! soul, poor soul of man! what heavenly fire
Would thrill thy depths and love of God inspire,
Could'st thou but see the Master hand revealed,
Majestic move "earth's scheme of things entire."

It cannot be! Unseen He guideth us
But yet our feeble hands, the luminous
Pure lamp of faith can light, to glorify
The narrow path that He has traced for us.

Sabbath—XXVIII

He will turn again, he will have compassion upon us; he will subdue our iniquities; and thou wilt cast all their sins into the depths of the sea.—MICAH vii. 19.

Search me, O God, and know my heart : try me, and know my thoughts : and see if there be any wicked way in me, and lead me in the way everlasting.—PSALM cxxxix. 23, 24.

DAWN

I ROSE at dawn to praise Thy name,
My sins o'erwhelmed my soul with shame,
But comfort after penance came,
For all my hopes are set in Thee.

Thou, O Almighty, knowest all
The passions that my heart enthrall,
Thy many mercies I recall,
And to Thy throne for refuge flee.

DAWN

No profit unto Thee it were
That I Thy chastening rod should bear,
Turn then, O Lord, and hear my prayer
And pardon mine iniquity.

To Thee my hope, my longings rise,
To Thee my soul for succour flies,
And I bewail my sins with sighs,
Like to the moaning of the sea.

Thy name puts all my cares to flight,
And radiates through my darkest night,
The thought of Thee is my delight,
And sweet as honey-comb to me.

Sabbath—XXIX

They that trust in the Lord shall be as mount Zion, which cannot be removed, but abideth for ever. As the mountains are round about Jerusalem, so the Lord is round about his people from henceforth even for ever.—PSALM cxxv. 1, 2.

Rejoice ye with Jerusalem, and be glad with her, all ye that love her: rejoice for joy with her, all ye that mourn for her: . . . As one whom his mother comforteth, so will I comfort you; and ye shall be comforted in Jerusalem.—ISAIAH lxvi. 10, 13.

HAPPY HE WHO SAW OF OLD

HAPPY he who saw of old
The high priest, with gems and gold
All adorned from crown to hem,
Tread thy courts, Jerusalem,
Till he reached the sacred place
Where the Lord's especial grace
Ever dwelt, the centre of the whole.
Happy he whose eyes
Saw at last the cloud of glory rise,
But to hear of it afflicts our soul.

Happy he that day who saw
How, with reverence and awe
And with sanctity of mien,
Spoke the priest: "Ye shall be clean
From your sins before the Lord,"
Echoed long the holy word,
While around the fragrant incense stole.
Happy he whose eyes
Saw at last the cloud of glory rise,
But to hear of it afflicts our soul.

Happy he who saw the crowd,
That in adoration bowed,
As they heard the priest proclaim,
"One, Ineffable, the Name,"
And they answered, "Blessed be
God, the Lord eternally,
He whom all created worlds extol."
Happy he whose eyes
Saw at last the cloud of glory rise,
But to hear of it afflicts our soul.

Happy he who saw the priest
Turn towards the shining east.
And, with solemn gladness thrilled,
Read the doctrine, that distilled
As the dew upon the plain,

As the showers of gentle rain,
While he raised on high the sacred scroll.
Happy he whose eyes
Saw at last the cloud of glory rise,
But to hear of it afflicts our soul.

Happy he who saw the walls
Of the temple's radiant halls,
Where the golden cherubim
Hide the ark's recesses dim,
Heard the singer's choral song,
Saw the Levites' moving throng,
Saw the golden censer and the bowl.
Happy he whose eyes
Saw at last the cloud of glory rise,
But to hear of it afflicts our soul.

Ever thus the burden rang
Of the pious songs, that sang
All the glories past and gone
Israel once did gaze upon,
Glories of the sacred fane,
Which they mourned and mourned again,
With a bitterness beyond control.
Happy he whose eyes
Saw (they said) the cloud of glory rise,
But to hear of it afflicts our soul.

Singers of a by-gone day
Who from earth have passed away,
Now ye see the glories shine
Of that distant land divine,
And no more (entranced by them)
Mourn this world's Jerusalem.
Happy ye who, from that heavenly goal,
See with other eyes,
Far, than ours, such radiant visions rise
That to hear of them delights our soul,

Sabbath—XXX

And now, Israel, what doth the Lord thy God require of thee, but to fear the Lord thy God, to walk in all his ways, and to love him, and to serve the Lord thy God with all thy heart and with all thy soul?—DEUTERONOMY x. 12.

O SLEEPER, WAKE, ARISE!

O SLEEPER, wake, arise!
Delusive follies shun,
Keep from the ways of men and raise thine eyes
To the exalted One.
Hasten as haste the starry orbs of gold
To serve the Rock of old.
O Sleeper, rise and call upon thy God!

Behold the firmament
His hands have wrought on high,
See how His mighty arms uphold the tent
Of His ethereal sky,

And mark the host of stars that heaven reveals,
His graven rings and seals.
Tremble before His majesty and hope
For His salvation still,
Lest, when for thee the gates of fortune ope,
False pride thy spirit fill.
O Sleeper, rise and call upon thy God!

Go seek at night abroad
Their footsteps, who erewhile
Were saints on earth, whose lips with hymns o'erflow'd
Whose hearts were free from guile.
Their nights were spent in ceaseless prayer and praise
In pious fasts their days.
Their souls were paths to God and by His throne
Their place is set anigh.
Their road through life was but a stepping-stone
Unto the Lord on high.
O Sleeper, rise and call upon thy God!

Whence does man's wisdom flow,
Man, who of dust is wrought,
Whose poor pre-eminence on earth does show
Over the beast as naught?
Only those gazing with the inward eye
Behold God's majesty:
They have the well-spring of their being found

More precious far than wine.
Thou also thus, though by earth's fetters bound,
May'st find thy Rock divine.
O Sleeper, rise and call upon thy God!

The Lord is Lord of all,
His hands hold life and death,
He bids the lowly rise, the lofty fall,
The world obeys his breath.
Keep judgment then, and live, and cast aside
False and rebellious pride
That asketh when and where, and all below
And all above, would know;
But be thou perfect with the Lord thy God!
O Sleeper, rise and call upon thy God!

Sabbath—XXXI

Except the Lord build the house, they labour in vain that build it: except the Lord keep the city, the watchman waketh but in vain. It is vain for you to rise up early, to sit up late, to eat the bread of sorrows: for so he giveth his beloved sleep.
—Psalm cxxvii. 1, 2.

AT EVENING

Cause us, our Father, to lie down in peace,
And raise us up, our King, to life again;
Direct us on our way
With Thy good counsel's stay
And let us 'neath Thy tent of peace remain.

O save us for the sake of Thy great name,
Be unto us a shield, Thou King of kings.
Remove from out our life
Sickness and care and strife,
Shelter us in the shadow of Thy wings.

Our guardian and deliverer Thou art,
Merciful king, whom heaven and earth adore!
Guard Thou from harm and sin
Our goings out and in,
With life and peace henceforth and evermore.

# Sabbath—XXXII

> I will praise thee, O Lord, with my whole heart; I will shew forth all thy marvellous works. I will be glad and rejoice in thee: I will sing praise to thy name, O thou most High.—Psalm ix. 1, 2.

PRAISE YE THE ALMIGHTY

Praise ye the Almighty,
Blessed be His name,
Sing the Rock, our Maker
And His might proclaim,
Through unnumbered ages
    Still the same.

Endless are the wonders,
That His hand has wrought,
Past the power of number,
Past the range of thought,
With exceeding glory
    Ever fraught.

Every living being
Doth His aid implore.
Bless ye then His greatness
And His name adore,
Ye His well-loved people,
    Evermore.

Lord of all creation,
God, supreme, most high,
Fount of life eternal,
Bless'd unceasingly,
With perpetual praises
    Sanctify.

Taste and see, ye children,
That the Lord is good,
Happy he, who trusting
In His fatherhood,
Terrors and temptations
    Has withstood.

Glorify and praise Him
And His power proclaim
Through unnumbered ages
Still the same.
Blessed through all ages
    Be His name.

Sabbath—XXXIII

Praise ye the Lord from the heavens: praise him in the heights. Praise ye him, all his angels: praise ye him, all his hosts. Praise ye him, sun and moon: praise him, all ye stars of light. Praise him, ye heavens of heavens, and ye waters that be above the heavens. Let them praise the name of the Lord: for he commanded, and they were created. . . . Let them praise the name of the Lord: for his name alone is excellent: his glory is above the earth and heaven.—PSALM cxlviii. 1-5, 13.

THE WONDERS OF GOD

FROM day to day, my soul, breathe forth thy prayer,
And in the watches of the night declare
His praises, who is clothed with majesty,
And girt about with wonders past compare.

His power and strength the universe pervade.
His presence fills this earth, that He has made,
Even as the cloud is filled with rain, that falls

On barren places, parched and void of shade,
Till leaves grow green and flowers bloom once more.
These are His wonders, His whom I adore,
He is my God, my refuge, and my rock,
To raise, to help, to gladden and restore.

He tells the stars the hour to shed their light,
Even as the flowers in spring-time blossom bright.
Like unto song-birds scattered o'er the plain
Are they, those wand'ring travellers of night,
That flee, before the sun at dawn appears.
With reverent awe, they bend their radiant spheres
Before their God, whose mighty hand upholds
The heavens and their shining tent uprears.
He binds and loosens all the starry horde,
He calls unto the heavens, and at His word
They melt, while ocean's seething depths arise
Tempestuous, at the summons of the Lord.

Thou uncreated One, creating all,
The mighty fear Thee none can Thee appal.
Who is there who can hide his path from Thee,
Or stand when Thou hast destined him to fall?
In bitterness of soul do I arise,
And unto Thee, enthroned above the skies,
I pray that it may be Thy will to grant

Forgiveness of my iniquities.
O! let me now the joyful tidings learn
That mercy has effaced thy judgment stern,
Thou Lord of all, whose mandate bringeth grief,
But whose swift word that grief to joy can turn.

Sabbath—XXXIV

Yet the number of the children of Israel shall be as the sand of the sea, which cannot be measured nor numbered.—HOSEA i. 10.

Blessed be the Lord, who daily loadeth us with benefits, even the God of our salvation.—PSALM lxviii. 19.

AS THE SAND OF THE SEA

MAY the Almighty bless, from age to age,
The seed of Israel, His heritage,
And lead back Judah to the promised land—
O may He make our numbers as the sand.

Now righteousness and peace, for ever bless'd,
Among this people, through long years oppress'd,
Embrace each other at the Lord's command.
O may He make our numbers as the sand.

Mercy and truth are met, and in our sight
They have drawn near to us to give us light.

O may His blessing rest upon our band,
And may He make our numbers as the sand.

The God of Israel your Saviour is,
And He will pardon your iniquities,
We will not, therefore, fear His chastening hand:
O may He make our numbers as the sand.

Return, ye faithful, to your rest once more,
With joyful song the Lord our God adore,
And bless and praise His name from land to land—
O may He make our numbers as the sand.

Sabbath—XXXV

The Lord bless thee, and keep thee : the Lord make his face shine upon thee, and be gracious unto thee : the Lord lift up his countenance upon thee, and give thee peace.—NUMBERS vi. 24-26.

Great peace have they which love thy law.—PSALM cxix. 165.

THE PEACE OF GOD

MOST blessed is, beyond compare,
The peace of God,
A crystal stream, that softly flows,
A shelter, when the storm-wind blows,
A star, whose light for ever glows.
The path we trod
So wearily, grows perfect fair
When heaven's own messenger is there—
The peace of God.

Sabbath—XXXVI

And the Lord, he it is that doth go before thee; he will be with thee, he will not fail thee, neither forsake thee: fear not, neither be dismayed.—DEUTERONOMY xxxi. 8.

My presence shall go with thee, and I will give thee rest.—EXODUS xxxiii. 14.

FAITH

Of all Thy gifts the best, O Lord, bestow
On us Thy needy people, sore distress'd,
Sore travel worn, and stained with sin and woe,
    Of all Thy gifts the best.

Then shall we find, amid life's toilsome quest,
The peace of God, from which all blessings flow,
Then shall no evil fears our souls molest.

Faith, faith in Thee, faith that, where'er we go,
Thy presence goes with us, and gives us rest,
That is in heaven above, on earth below,
    Of all Thy gifts the best!

Sabbath—XXXVII

For thus saith the high and lofty One that inhabiteth eternity, whose name is Holy; I dwell in the high and holy place, with him also that is of a contrite and humble spirit, to revive the spirit of the humble, and to revive the heart of the contrite ones.—ISAIAH lvii. 15.

O THOU RED SEA!

O THOU Red Sea and Sinai! make known
Where my Beloved has gone,
What path He has decreed,
Then to the palace of my Lord with speed
I will go forth, and sheltered in His breast
Find there at last tranquillity and rest.
Horeb, thou mount of God, I ask of thee
Declare if ever He
Unto thy holy seer
Did in the burning bush again appear.
O'er all the world, His footstool and His throne,
I pass and ask, but answer is there none.

Midst all my griefs and sorrows multiplied,
Does He perchance abide
Within my heart to prove
How sure a refuge is His heavenly love?
Yea, I have found Him there, my shield and stay,
He helped me, and my sorrows passed away.
Balm is it to my wound to find that He
Thus closely holdeth me.
Nor will I e'er demand
A kingdom, nay, nor Judah's promised land.
If but within my soul I feel and know
His loving kindnesses' unceasing flow,
When on my tongue withal
His words of love like drops of honey fall,
Weakened and humble grows
The sinful pride, that in my heart arose.
He is to me a crown, a diadem;
Why should I then desire gold or gem?

O my Beloved, whom I have ever known
I long for Thee alone,
And through my love for Thee,
My foes, in bitter wrath, have exiled me.
But if, 'midst all, I should forget Thee, let
My right hand, Lord, her cunning then forget.
May'st Thou, my Father and my King, restore
Thy temple as of yore,

O THOU RED SEA!

Thy scattered flock behold,
And gather them into Thy sheltering fold;
Thy covenant establish, O Most High,
And make Thine ear attentive to our cry.
The dove, at the grave's mouth who builds her nest,
Lead in Thy courts to rest.
As in the ancient days,
Renew my joy, pour forth Thy glory's rays,
Return once more unto Thy sacred shrine,
And shed o'er me again Thy light divine.

Sabbath—XXXVIII

Boast not thyself of to-morrow; for thou knowest not what a day may bring forth.—PROVERBS xxvii. 1.

HILLEL AND HIS GUEST

HILLEL, the gentle, the beloved sage,
Expounded day by day the sacred page
To his disciples in the house of learning;
And day by day, when home at eve returning,
They lingered, clust'ring round him, loth to part
From him whose gentle rule won every heart.
But evermore, when they were wont to plead
For longer converse, forth he went with speed,
Saying each day: "I go—the hour is late—
To tend the guest who doth my coming wait,"
Until at last they said: "The Rabbi jests
When telling us thus daily of his guests
That wait for him." The Rabbi paused awhile,
And then made answer: "Think you I beguile

You with an idle tale? Not so, forsooth!
I have a guest, whom I must tend in truth.
Is not the soul of man indeed a guest,
Who in this body deigns a while to rest,
And dwells with me all peacefully to-day:
To-morrow—may it not have fled away?"

Sabbath—XXXIX

The Lord shall preserve thy going out and thy coming in, from this time forth, and even for evermore.—Psalm cxxi. 8.

He that dwelleth in the secret place of the Most High, shall abide under the shadow of the Almighty.—Psalm xci. 1.

PARAPHRASE OF PSALM CXXI

Unto the hills I lift mine eyes,
Whence comes my help, my help that lies
In God, enthroned above the skies,
Who made the heavens and earth to be.

He guides thy foot o'er mountain steeps,
He slumbers not, thy soul who keeps,
Behold He slumbers not, nor sleeps,
Of Israel the guardian He.

He is thy rock, thy shield and stay,
On thy right hand a shade alway,

The sun ne'er smiteth thee by day,
The moon at night ne'er troubles thee.

The Lord will guard thy soul from sin,
Thy life from harm without, within,
Thy going out and coming in,
From this time forth eternally.

Sabbath—XL

Shew me thy ways, O Lord : teach me thy paths.—Psalm xxv. 4.

All the paths of the Lord are mercy and truth unto such as keep his covenant and his testimonies.—Psalm xxv. 10.

THE WAYS OF GOD

Fair in mine eyes are all Thy ways,
And sweet it is to walk therein,
For there man stumbles not, nor strays,
There is no pitfall, snare, or sin.
      There do I move
With gladness, drawn to Thee by bonds of love.

Fountain of life, my soul's desire,
My hope and refuge, Thou Most High,
To see Thy glory I aspire,
Too great a bliss for such as I;
      Thus when I yearn
For Thee, unto Thy house my steps I turn.

O be Thy love my shield and stay!
Strengthen my heart to serve Thee still,
Then shall Thine anger pass away,
For I have not transgressed Thy will.
     My chief delight
Is in Thy law, my study day and night.

The favour of Thy countenance
Strengthened my arm in days of yore,
Thy service mine inheritance
Has been, and shall be evermore.
     Thou leadest me,
Yea, though Thou slay me, I will trust in Thee.

Sabbath—XLI

In all ages entering into holy souls, she (Wisdom) maketh them friends of God and prophets.—WISDOM OF SOLOMON vii. 27.

THE SOUL

LORD, my soul athirst for Thee
Liveth but Thy light to see,
Though consumed with longing, lives,
For new life that longing gives.
Made in God's similitude,
And with heavenly powers endued.
In His steps she followeth,
Seeking Him with every breath,
Passing free through boundless space,
All untouched by time or place,
Executing her intent
Without tool or instrument

THE SOUL

When the body's frame decay'd
In the gloomy grave is laid,
Then the soul with joyful might
Heavenward takes her radiant flight,
Serving God her sole delight.
Earthly treasures she forsakes,
And a bond of union makes
With the angels of the Lord,
One with them in sweet accord.
Endless is the good she sees,
All celestial harmonies,
Joy and everlasting pleasure,
More and more beyond all measure.

Sabbath—XLII

Commit thy way unto the Lord; trust also in him, and he shall bring it to pass. And he shall bring forth thy righteousness as the light, and thy judgment as the noonday. Rest in the Lord, and wait patiently for him.—PSALM xxxvii. 5-7.

COMMIT THY WAY

COMMIT thy way unto the Lord, and trust
In Him. Poor soul, midst doubts and fears astray,
Dost thou in truth to Him, the wise and just,
    Commit thy way?

Dost thou not rather vainly strive to sway
To-morrow's fate, and at each stormy gust
Of fortune sink in measureless dismay?

Rest in the Lord, wait patiently, nor thrust
Forth feeble hands in vain, but day by day
To Him who lifts the needy from the dust
    Commit thy way!

Sabbath—XLIII

Remember now thy Creator in the days of thy youth, while the evil days come not, nor the years draw nigh, when thou shalt say, I have no pleasure in them. . . . Then shall the dust return to the earth as it was ; and the spirit shall return unto God who gave it.—ECCLESIASTES xii. 1, 7.

PRAYER

Unto thy Rock, my soul, uplift thy gaze,
His loving-kindness day and night implore.
Remember thy Creator in the days
Of youth, in song His glorious name adore.
He is thy portion through earth's troubled maze,
Thy shelter, when life's pilgrimage is o'er.
Thou knowest that there waits for thee always
A peaceful resting-place His throne before.
Therefore the Lord my God I bless and praise,
Even as all creatures bless Him evermore.

Sabbath—XLIV

I wait for the Lord, my soul doth wait, and in his word do I hope. My soul waiteth for the Lord more than they that watch for the morning: I say, more than they that watch for the morning.—Psalm cxxx. 5, 6.

YEA, MORE THAN THEY

Yea, more than they, who through the gloomy night,
Through sleepless hours, that loiter on their way,
Watch for the dawn above the eastern height,
    Yea, more than they.

Watching and waiting for return of day,
My soul waits for the Lord, the Lord of might,
With whom forgiveness is, my hope and stay.

And when His mercy thrills my soul contrite,
My soul rejoices in His pardoning ray,
More than they joy to see the morning light,
    Yea, more than they.

Sabbath—XLV

As thy days, so shall thy strength be.—DEUTERONOMY xxxiii. 25.

So teach us to number our days, that we may apply our hearts unto wisdom.—PSALM xc. 12.

AT MORNING

O LORD, my life was known to Thee
Ere Thou had'st caused me yet to be,
Thy spirit ever dwells in me.

Could I, cast down by Thee, have gained
A standing place, or, if restrained
By Thee, go forth with feet unchained?

Hear me, Almighty, while I pray,
My thoughts are in Thy hand alway,
Be to my helplessness a stay!

O! may this hour Thy favour yield
And may I tread life's battle-field
Encompassed by Thy mercy's shield.

Wake me at dawn Thy name to bless,
And in Thy sanctuary's recess
To praise and laud Thy holiness.

Sabbath—XLVI

Unto you that fear my name shall the Sun of righteousness arise with healing in his wings.—MALACHI iv. 2.

O send out thy light and thy truth: let them lead me.—PSALM xliii. 3.

When I sit in darkness, the Lord shall be a light unto me.—MICAH vii. 8.

O LORD, I CALL ON THEE

O LORD, I call on Thee when sore dismayed,
And Thou wilt hear my voice and lend me aid,
Nor shall I be of myriads afraid,
For Thou wilt ever be
The portion of my lot—Thou savest me.

In troubled times Thy mercy's plenteous store
Is full to overflowing evermore,
And when in straitness I my plaint outpour,
With words entreating Thee,
Then with enlargement Thou dost answer me.

Make known Thy love to those who trust and pray,
To those, who hold Thy name their help and stay,
Waiting for Thy salvation day by day.
Yea, who, O Lord, but Thee,
Shall make me glad, who else deliver me?

Do Thou from heavenly heights my pain behold,
And lead me back unto Thy sheltering fold,
That I may answer scorners as of old:
Yea, though my dwelling be
In darkest night, God is a light to me.

Sabbath—XLVII

But the souls of the righteous are in the hand of God, and there shall no torment touch them. In the sight of the unwise they seemed to die, and their departure is taken for misery and their going from us to be utter destruction : but they are in peace.—WISDOM OF SOLOMON iii. 1-3.

SOULS OF THE RIGHTEOUS

SOULS of the righteous—in God's hand they lie
Untouched by shadows from the pilgrim land,
No pain, or torment ever cometh nigh
Souls of the righteous in God's hand.

Such peace is theirs earth cannot understand,
Although to the unwise they seemed to die,
They are at rest, a holy, blessed band.

Like to the stars, whose radiant galaxy
Gleams in the tent of heaven o'er us spann'd,
So shine, among His angels set on high,
Souls of the righteous in God's hand.

Sabbath—XLVIII

Happy is the man that findeth wisdom, and the man that getteth understanding. . . . Her ways are ways of pleasantness and all her paths are peace.—PROVERBS iii. 13, 17.

The path of the just is as the shining light, that shineth more and more unto the perfect day.—PROVERBS iv. 18.

HOW LONG

How long wilt thou in childhood's slumber lie?
Know that youth flies like chaff the wind before.
Can spring for ever last? Nay, soon draws nigh
Old age's messenger, with tresses hoar.
Shake thyself free from sin, as ere they fly,
The birds shake off the night-dews' pearled store.
Cast off temptations, that thy peace defy,
Like troubled waves upon a rocky shore,
And follow after that pure company
Of souls, that seek God's goodness evermore.

Sabbath—XLIX

When thou cuttest down thine harvest in thy field, and hast forgot a sheaf in the field, thou shalt not go again to fetch it : it shall be for the stranger, for the fatherless, and for the widow : that the Lord thy God may bless thee in all the work of thy hands.—DEUTERONOMY xxiv. 19.

THE COMMANDMENT OF FORGETFULNESS

RABBI ben Zadok, o'er the sacred law
Bending with reverent joy, with holy awe,
Read the commandment : " When thy harvest yields
Its fruit and thou, when reaping in thy fields,
Dost there forget a sheaf of golden grain,
Fetch it not in to thee. It shall remain—
The poor, the stranger and the widow's store.
And the Lord God shall bless thee evermore."
Rabbi ben Zadok closed the well-loved book,
And, gazing upward with a troubled look,
He said : " With joy do I obey, O Lord,

Each hest and precept of Thy holy word,
For which Thy name at morn and eve I bless,
But this commandment of forgetfulness
I have not yet performed as Thou hast willed,
Since to remember leaves it unfulfilled."
So mused the Rabbi. But when autumn came,
And waves of corn glowed 'neath the sunset's flame,
It chanced at evening, that, his labours o'er,
He stood and gazed upon his garnered store,
And suddenly to him his little son
Came saying: "Father, see what thou hast done!
Three sheaves in yonder field I have espied
Forgotten!" "Oh!" the pious rabbi cried,
"Blessed art Thou, O Lord, whose gracious will
Enables me Thy bidding to fulfil,
Even through some oversight." And with the day
Unto the house of God he took his way,
And offered of his flocks and herds the best,
For joy to have obeyed the Lord's behest.

Thus runs the Talmud tale! O God, may we
Thus evermore rejoice in serving Thee.

Sabbath—L

I will both lay me down in peace and sleep : for thou, Lord, only makest me dwell in safety.—PSALM iv. 8.

Thou wilt keep him in perfect peace, whose mind is stayed on thee : because he trusteth in thee.—ISAIAH xxvi. 3.

FROM PSALM IV

OFFER the sacrifice of righteousness,
And put thy trust for evermore
In the Lord God of Hosts, whose name we bless,
    Whose mercy we adore.

Many there be that say : Yea, who shall show
Us any good in coming years?
And on the burden of to-day they throw
    To-morrow's doubts and fears.

Lord, lift Thou up o'er us Thy countenance,
And let its light shine on our way,

Then shall we move, unharmed by time and chance,
  With Thee our help and stay.

Thou hast put gladness in my heart yet more
Than when their corn and wine increased,
For little need we seek for earthly store,
  By Thee from care released.

I will both lay me down in peace and sleep,
For Thou alone dost make me dwell
In safety, Thou who dost Thy children keep,
  And orderest all things well.

Sabbath—LI

But now, O Lord, thou art our father; we are the clay and thou our potter; and we all are the work of thy hand.—ISAIAH lxiv. 8.

Ye stand this day all of you before the Lord your God. . . . That thou shouldest enter into covenant with the Lord thy God, and into his oath, which the Lord thy God maketh with thee this day: that he may establish thee to-day for a people unto himself, and that he may be unto thee a God, as he hath said unto thee, and as he hath sworn unto thy fathers, to Abraham, to Isaac, and to Jacob.—DEUTERONOMY xxix. 10, 12, 13.

LO, AS THE POTTER

Lo, as the potter moulds his clay
Shaping and forming it from day to day,
Thus in Thy hand, O Lord, are we.
O Thou whose mercies never pass away,
Forgive our sins once more,
And keep Thy covenant as in days of yore.

Even as the mason hews the stone,
And one is carved and wrought, and shattered one,
Thus in Thy hand, O Lord, are we,
Thou who of life and death art Lord alone.
Forgive our sins once more,
And keep Thy covenant as in days of yore.

Lo, as amidst the fiery glow
The smith his iron forges blow on blow,
Thus in Thy hand, O Lord, are we,
O Thou who savest those by care laid low,
Forgive our sins once more,
And keep Thy covenant as in days of yore.

Even as the helm the steerman's hand
Holdeth now firmly grasped, now lightly spann'd,
Thus in Thy hand, O Lord, are we;
O Thou who pardonest the transgressor's band,
Forgive our sins once more,
And keep Thy covenant as in days of yore.

Lo, as the artificer's breath
Now forms, now melts the glass he fashioneth,
Thus in Thy hand, O Lord, are we;
O Thou whose love our weakness succoureth,
Forgive our sins once more
And keep Thy covenant as in days of yore.

Lo, as the silver seven times tried
Is in the smelter's furnace purified,
Thus in Thy hand, O Lord, are we;
O Thou, who balm and healing scatterest wide,
Forgive our sins once more,
And keep Thy covenant as in days of yore.

Sabbath—LII

Seek ye the Lord while he may be found, call ye upon him while he is near : let the wicked forsake his way, and the unrighteous man his thoughts : and let him return unto the Lord, and he will have mercy upon him ; and to our God, for he will abundantly pardon. For my thoughts are not your thoughts, neither are your ways my ways, saith the Lord. For as the heavens are higher than the earth, so are my ways higher than your ways, and my thoughts than your thoughts.—ISAIAH lv. 6-9.

PENITENTIAL PRAYER

FORTH flies my soul upborne by hope untiring
The land of rest, the spring of life desiring,
Unto the heavenly dwelling-place aspiring,
To seek its peace by day and night.

My spirit does God's majesty adore,
And without wings shall to His presence soar,
There to behold His glory evermore,
At dawn, at noonday, and at night.

On all His works mine eye in wonder gazes,
And heavenward an eager look upraises;
Day unto day proclaims its Maker's praises,
And night declares them unto night.

Thy loving-kindness is my life-long guide,
But often from Thy path I've turned aside.
O Lord, how hast Thou searched my heart, and tried
My inmost thoughts at dead of night.

Sleepless, upon my bed the hours I number,
And, rising, seek the house of God, while slumber
Lies heavy on men's eyes and dreams encumber
Their souls in visions of the night.

In sin and folly passed my early years,
Wherefore I am ashamed, and life's arrears
Now strive to pay, the while my bitter tears
Have been my food by day and night.

Pent in the body's cage, pure child of heaven,
Bethink thee, life but as a bridge is given.
Awake, arise, to praise God gladly, even
In the first hours of the night.

Haste then, pure heart, to break sin's deadly sway,
And seek the path of righteousness alway;

For all our years are but as yesterday—
Soon past, and as a watch at night.

Short is man's life, and full of care and sorrow,
This way and that he turns some ease to borrow,
Like to a flower he blooms, and on the morrow
Is gone—a vision of the night.

How does the weight of sin my soul oppress,
Because God's law too often I transgress;
I mourn and sigh, with tears of bitterness
My bed I water all the night.

I rise at dawn and still the salt stream flows,
My heart's blood would I shed to find repose;
But when my soul is downcast with my woes,
I will recall my prayer at night.

My youth wanes like a shadow that is cast,
Swifter than eagle's wings my years fly fast,
And I remember not my gladness past,
Either by day or yet by night.

Proclaim we then a fast, a holy day,
Make pure our hearts from sin, God's will obey,
And unto Him, with humbled spirit, pray
Unceasingly, by day and night.

May we yet hear His words : "Thou art my own,
My grace is thine, the shelter of My throne,
For I am thy Redeemer, I alone ;
Endure but patiently this night!"

Sabbath—LIII

And the Lord spake unto Moses that selfsame day, saying, Get thee up into this mountain Abarim, unto mount Nebo, which is in the land of Moab, that is over against Jericho ; and behold the land of Canaan, which I give unto the children of Israel for a possession : and die in the mount whither thou goest up, and be gathered unto thy people ; as Aaron thy brother died in mount Hor, and was gathered unto his people.— DEUTERONOMY xxxii. 48-50.

THE DEATH OF MOSES

THIS the road I tread to-day
God has ordered, I obey,
Far from all I take my way,
O my people, be at peace.

What we do we know not; still
God His pleasure does fulfil,
And none questioneth His will.
Thou, our shepherd, go in peace.

THE DEATH OF MOSES

Now the parting hour is nigh,
The appointed time, and I,
Even as Aaron died, shall die,
O my people, be at peace.

Lo the path that thou must tread,
Whither great and small are led,
Who is there that does not dread?
Thou, our shepherd, go in peace,

God it is who spake to me:
Yonder mount thy death shall see,
Sad was I exceedingly.
O my people be at peace.

Death for all in ambush lies,
Yea, but precious in His eyes
Is it when His loved one dies:
Thou, our shepherd, go in peace.

Grief and care have laid me low,
For death's fatal touch I know.
Ah! and whither shall I go?
O my people, be at peace.

Be no more disconsolate,
For beyond death's gloomy gate,

Eden's joys thy coming wait.
Thou, our shepherd, go in peace.

How art thou, my soul, cast down!
From my head is fallen the crown,
Rent the rock of my renown.
O my people, be at peace.

'Midst God's angels thou shalt shine,
Grace and mercy shall be thine,
And eternal life divine.
Thou, our shepherd, go in peace.

Sabbath—LIV

There is none like unto the God of Jeshurun, who rideth upon the heaven in thy help, and in his excellency on the sky. The eternal God is thy refuge, and underneath are the everlasting arms.—DEUTERONOMY xxxiii. 26, 27.

HYMN OF GLORY

SWEET hymns and songs will I indite
To sing of Thee by day and night,
Of Thee, who art my soul's delight.

How doth my soul within me yearn
Beneath Thy shadow to return,
Thy secret mysteries to learn.

And even while yet Thy glory fires
My words, and hymns of praise inspires
Thy love it is my heart desires.

Therefore will I of Thee relate
All glorious things, and celebrate
In songs of love Thy name most great.

Thy glory shall my discourse be,
In images I picture Thee,
Although Thyself I cannot see.

In mystic utterances alone,
By prophet and by seer made known,
Hast Thou Thy radiant glory shown.

Thy might and greatness they portrayed
According to the power displayed
In all the works Thy hand has made.

In images of Thee they told,
Of Thy great wonders wrought of old,
Thy essence could they not behold.

In signs and visions seen of yore
They pictured Thee in ancient lore,
But Thou art One for evermore.

They saw in Thee both youth and age,
The man of war, the hoary sage,
But ever Israel's heritage.

O Thou whose word is truth alway,
Thy people seek Thy face this day,
O be Thou near them when they pray.

May these, my songs and musings, be
Acceptable, O Lord, to Thee,
And do Thou hear them graciously.

O let my praises heavenward sped,
Be as a crown unto Thy head.
My prayer as incense offeréd!

O may my words of blessing rise
To Thee, who throned above the skies,
Art just and mighty, great and wise!

And when Thy glory I declare
Do Thou incline Thee to my prayer,
As though sweet spice my offering were.

My meditation day and night,
May it be pleasant in Thy sight,
For Thou art all my soul's delight.

WHEN THE MORNING CAME

(Hymn for the First Day of Passover)

The Glory of the Lord our God behold,
Who set us free from bondage sore,
And praise in song the mercies manifold
He grants us evermore.
When close and closer dangers thee appal
And fill with terror day and night,
O bid thy heart remember midst them all
That darkness turns to light.
Mark how the sun now rising golden clear
Sank yester eve in gloomy gray,—
Then wherefore let to-morrow's doubt and fear
    Afflict thy soul to-day?

Look up unto our help in ages past,
In troubled days and perilous,
What time the hostile camps besieged us fast,
And nigh consuméd us.

O silent Dove, the glorious power await
Of Him who doth thy life redeem,
Who makes the men of might, their pomp and state,
As passing shadows seem ;
Then like a vision of the night is stilled
The haughty tumult of the foe,
And all the pride with which his heart is filled
    Is suddenly brought low.

Declare then evermore unweariedly
To generations yet unknown,
The wonders that our Rock in majesty
Has to His people shown.
Seek'st thou a sign to know the dead once more
Shall rise to life, their troubles past,
And that earth's pilgrims, all their wand'rings o'er,
Shall dwell in peace at last?
Look upon this—how God from out the grave
Did lead us forth to life and breath,
And how He wrought great miracles to save
    Us from the dust of death

Therefore with closéd lips and silent tongue,
Accept thine hour of sore distress,
And banish from thy heart, by anguish wrung,
All wrath and bitterness.
Hope still for happier days. To every woe

Shall come an end, though long delayed.
Why is thy hand grown slack, thy faith sunk low?
Be strong and undismayed.
Remember how one evening saw of old
A nation plunged in darkest night,
And when the morning came again—behold,
    The Lord had brought us light!

BY THE RED SEA

(HYMN FOR THE SEVENTH DAY OF PASSOVER)

WHEN as a wall the sea
In heaps uplifted lay,
A new song unto Thee
    Sang the redeemed that day.

Thou didst in his deceit
O'erwhelm the Egyptian's feet,
While Israel's footsteps fleet
    How beautiful were they!

Jeshurun! all who see
Thy glory cry to Thee
"Who like thy God can be?"
    Thus even our foes did say.

O let thy banner soar
The scattered remnant o'er,
And gather them once more,
    Like corn on harvest-day.

Who bear through all their line
Thy covenant's holy sign,
And to Thy name divine
    Are sanctified alway.

Let all the world behold
Their token prized of old,
Who on their garment's fold
    The thread of blue display.

Be then the truth made known
For whom, and whom alone,
The twisted fringe is shown,
    The covenant kept this day.

O let them, sanctified,
Once more with Thee abide,
Their sun shine far and wide,
    And chase the clouds away.

The well-beloved declare
Thy praise in song and prayer :

"Who can with Thee compare,
   O Lord of Hosts?" they say.

When as a wall the sea
In heaps uplifted lay,
A new song unto Thee
   Sang the redeemed that day.

SINAI

(Hymn for Pentecost)

When Thou didst descend upon Sinai's mountain,
It trembled and shook 'neath Thy mighty hand,
And the rocks were moved by Thy power and splendour:
How then can my spirit before Thee stand
On the day when darkness o'erspread the heavens
And the sun was hidden at Thy command?
The angels of God, for Thy great name's worship,
Are ranged before Thee, a shining band,
And the children of men are awaiting ever
Thy mercies unnumbered as grains of sand;
The law they received from the mouth of Thy glory
They learn and consider and understand.
O accept Thou their song and rejoice in their gladness,
Who proclaim Thy glory in every land.

ODE TO ZION

(HYMN FOR THE FAST OF AB)

ART thou not, Zion, fain
To send forth greetings from thy sacred rock
Unto thy captive train,
Who greet thee as the remnants of thy flock?
Take Thou on every side,
East, west and south and north, their greetings multiplied.
Sadly he greets thee still,
The prisoner of hope who, day and night,
Sheds ceaseless tears, like dew on Hermon's hill.
Would that they fell upon thy mountain's height!

Harsh is my voice, when I bewail thy woes,
But when in fancy's dream
I see thy freedom, forth its cadence flows,

Sweet as the harps, that hung by Babel's stream.
My heart is sore distressed
For Bethel ever blessed,
For Peniel and each ancient, sacred place.
The holy presence there
To thee is present, where
Thy Maker opes thy gates, the gates of heaven to face.

The glory of the Lord will ever be
Thy sole and perfect light:
No need hast thou then, to illumine thee,
Of sun by day, or moon and stars by night.
I would that, where God's spirit was of yore
Poured out unto thy holy ones, I might
There too my soul outpour.
The house of kings and throne of God wert thou,
How comes it then that now
Slaves fill the throne where sat thy kings before?

Oh, who will lead me on
To seek the spots where, in far distant years,
The angels in their glory dawned upon
Thy messengers and seers?
Oh, who will give me wings
That I may fly away,
And there, at rest from all my wanderings,
The ruins of my heart among thy ruins lay?

ODE TO ZION

I'll bend my face unto thy soil, and hold
Thy stones as precious gold.
And when in Hebron I have stood beside
My fathers' tombs, then will I pass in turn
Thy plains and forest wide,
Until I stand on Gilead and discern
Mount Hor and Mount Abarim, 'neath whose crest
Thy luminaries twain, thy guides and beacons rest.

Thy air is life unto my soul, thy grains
Of dust are myrrh, thy streams with honey flow:
Naked and barefoot, to thy ruined fanes
How gladly would I go:
To where the ark was treasured, and in dim
Recesses dwelt the holy cherubim.

I rend the beauty of my locks, and cry
In bitter wrath against the cruel fate
That bids thy holy Nazarites to lie
In earth contaminate.
How can I make of meat or drink my care?
How can mine eyes enjoy
The light of day, when I see ravens tear
Thy eagle's flesh, and dogs thy lions' whelps destroy?
Away, thou cup of sorrow's poisoned gall!
Scarce can my soul thy bitterness sustain.
When I Ahola unto mind recall,

I taste the venom: and when once again
Upon Aholiba I muse, thy dregs I drain.

Perfect in beauty, Zion, how in thee
Do love and grace unite!
The souls of thy companions tenderly
Turn unto thee: thy joy was their delight,
And weeping they lament thy ruin now.
In distant exile, for thy sacred height
They long, and towards thy gates in prayer they bow.
Thy flocks are scattered o'er the barren waste,
Yet do they not forget thy sheltering fold,
Unto thy garments' fringe they cling, and haste
The branches of thy palms to seize and hold.

Shinar and Pathros! come they near to thee?
Naught are they by thy light and right divine.
To what can be compared the majesty
Of thy anointed line?
To what the singers, seers, and Levites thine?
The rule of idols fails and is cast down;
Thy power eternal is, from age to age thy crown.

The Lord desires thee for His dwelling-place
Eternally, and bless'd
Is he whom God has chosen for the grace
Within thy courts to rest.

Happy is he that watches, drawing near,
Until he sees thy glorious lights arise,
And over whom thy dawn breaks full and clear
Set in the orient skies.
But happiest he, who, with exultant eyes,
The bliss of thy redeemed ones shall behold,
And see thy youth renewed as in the days of old.

MY KING

(Hymn for New Year)

Ere time began, ere age to age had thrilled,
I waited in His storehouse, as He willed;
He gave me being, but, my years fulfilled,
   I shall be summoned back before the King.

He called the hidden to the light of day,
To right and left, each side the fountain lay,
From out the stream and down the steps, the way
   That led me to the garden of the King.

Thou gavest me a light my path to guide,
To prove my heart's recesses still untried;
And as I went, Thy voice in warning cried:
   "Child, fear thou Him who is thy God and King!"

True weight and measure learned my heart from Thee :
If blessings follow, then what joy for me !
If naught but sin, all mine the shame must be,
  For that was not determined by the King.

I hasten, trembling, to confess the whole
Of my transgressions, ere I reach the goal
Where mine own words must witness 'gainst my soul,
  And who dares doubt the writing of the King ?

Erring, I wandered in the wilderness,
In passion's grave nigh sinking powerless :
Now deeply I repent, in sore distress,
  That I kept not the statutes of the King !

With worldly longings was my bosom fraught,
Earth's idle toys and follies all I sought :
Ah, when He judges joys so dearly bought,
  How greatly shall I fear my Lord and King !

Now conscience-stricken, humbled to the dust,
Doubting himself, in Thee alone his trust,
He shrinks in terror back, for God is just—
  How can a sinner hope to reach the King ?

Oh, be Thy mercy in the balance laid,
To hold Thy servant's sins more lightly weighed,

When, his confession penitently made,
    He answers for his guilt before the King.

Thine is the love, O God, and Thine the grace,
That folds the sinner in its mild embrace:
Thine the forgiveness bridging o'er the space
    'Twixt man's works and the task set by the King.

Unheeding all my sins, I cling to Thee;
I know that mercy will Thy footstool be:
Before I call, O do Thou answer me,
    For nothing dare I claim of Thee, my King!

O Thou who makest guilt to disappear,
My help, my hope, my rock, I will not fear:
Though Thou the body hold in dungeon drear,
    The soul has found the palace of the King.

JUDGMENT AND MERCY

(Hymn for New Year)

By the faithful of His children in their conclaves
Shall His name be sanctified;
Awe-inspiring are the praises of His angels,
And the voices in His temple spread His glory
      Far and wide.

Those who keep His law shall yet again be gathered
To the stronghold of His might,
Those who fear Him commune, praying, with each
    other—
He will hear and in the book of their memorial
      He will write.

Let your deeds be fair and righteous—then unbroken
He the covenant will hold.
He who maketh bright the heavens, He will heed you,

And will count your prayers more precious than the
    off'rings
        Brought of old.

May the tribes of those who worship and proclaim
    Him
Be uplifted as of yore;
When He pruneth, may He cut the straggling
    branches,
For to Him belong the sov'reignty and kingdom
        Evermore.

May He lead us once again unto the mountain
Of His sanctuary's shrine,
There to glorify Him ever in His Temple,
For our God will not forget His word, the holy
        And divine.

At His name shall heaven and earth break forth in
    praises
With a joy that shall not cease,
And the woods shall shout and clap their hands in
    gladness,
For the Lord our God has visited His people,
        Bringing peace.

From each band of angels mighty in their splendour,
From each shining, circling star,
Hymns and praises evermore declare His glory,
Saying: "Praise Him with the sound of joyful trumpets,
   The Shophar!"

All the creatures of the universe together,
Heaven above and earth below,
Shall proclaim, "The Lord in all His works is mighty,
He is King o'er all the earth, and His salvation
   All shall know."

THE ROYAL CROWN

(For the Penitential Days)

PART I

I

Wondrous are Thy works, O Lord of Hosts,
And their greatness holds my soul in thrall;
Thine the glory is, the power divine,
Thine the majesty, the kingdom Thine;
Thou supreme, exalted over all.

Thine is the throne in heavenly heights sublime,
The hidden dwelling-place all worlds above,
Th' existence, from the shadow of whose light
Springs every living thing, of which aright
We say, that in its shade we live and move.

Thine the two worlds, that thou dost hold apart,
The first for work, the next for heavenly rest:
Thine the reward, which Thou hast treasured there,
Wrought for the righteous ones, with loving care,
Because Thou hast beheld and known it blest.

II

Thou art One, the first great cause of all,
Thou art One, and none can penetrate,
Not even the wise in heart, the mystery
Of Thy unfathomable Unity:
Thou art One, the infinitely great.

III

Thou dost exist, but not the hearing ear
Or seeing eye can reach Thee: what Thou art,
And how and wherefore, is to us unknown.
Thou dost exist, but through Thyself alone,
King, in whose power no other has a part.

Thou dost exist: Thou wast ere time began,
Pervading all, when there was yet no space,
Thou dost exist: Thy mystery, concealed
Far from men's sight lies ever unrevealed,
Deep, deep, where none can find its dwelling-place.

IV

Thou livest, but not with the twofold life
Of soul and mind: soul of the soul art Thou.
Thou livest, and eternal joy shall bless,
At th' end of days, those whom Thy graciousness
To penetrate Thy mystery will allow.

V

Thou art mighty, and of all Thy works
There is none whose power to Thine comes nigh.
Thou art mighty, and Thy boundless power
Makes Thee pardon, even in the hour
Of Thy wrath, man's sore iniquity.

VI

Thou art light: pure souls shall Thee behold,
Save when mists of evil intervene.
Thou art light, that, in this world concealed,
In the world to come shall be revealed:
In the mount of God it shall be seen.

VII

Thou art God, and all whom Thou hast formed
Serve and worship Thee in love and fear:

Nor aught lessens it Thy majesty,
That they worship others besides Thee,
For they all would fain to Thee draw near.

Yet like blind men from the path they stray,
While they seek the great King's road to gain.
In destructive pits and snares they lie,
Ever deeming their desire is nigh,
Though they toil and labour all in vain.

But Thy servants move with open eyes,
On the straight path ever travelling,
Nor to right or left on either hand
Turn they, till within the court they stand,
Leading to the palace of the King.

Thou art God, and Thy Divinity
And Thy Unity the world uphold.
Thou art God, eternal, one, divine:
These, Thy attributes in Thee combine
Indivisible, yet manifold.

VIII

Thou art wise, and at Thy side hast reared
Wisdom, fount of life, Thy first-born son.
Thou art wise: this universal frame

At Thy mighty word to being came,
When to aid or counsel Thee was none.

Thou didst span the heaven's vast canopy
And the planet's shining tent uprear,
In Thy hand dost Thou, O Lord of might,
All creation's utmost ends unite,
Gathered as one whole from sphere to sphere.

PARTS II AND III

I

BEYOND conception great
Thy power is, wherewith Thou didst create
From out Thy glory's depths a radiant flame,
Hewn from the rock of rocks and wrought
Out of eternity, with wisdom fraught,
The soul, the living soul,—thus didst Thou call its
    name—
By Thee, Omnipotent,
Formed of the spirit's fire, and sent
To guard and keep and serve awhile this earthly
    frame.

Beyond all recompense,
O Lord our God, is Thy beneficence,
In that Thou didst enshrine
Within the body's cage the soul, that gift divine,
To give man life and light,
From evil rescue him and lead his steps aright.

Beyond all mysteries,
Lord, of Thy wondrous works the secret lies,
In that Thou gavest man
The power of sight Thy mighty world to scan,
Gavest the listening ear
Of all Thy glorious miracles to hear,
The mind to apprehend
A portion of Thy wonders without end,
And speech wherewith to praise
Thy works, and tell of all Thy wondrous ways.
   Lo! even thus do I,
Son of Thy handmaid, with humility
And faltering lips, proclaim
How Thou exalted art, how glorious is Thy name.

II

Shame-stricken, bending low,
My God, I come before Thee, for I know
That even as Thou on high

Exalted art in power and majesty,
So weak and frail am I,
That perfect as Thou art,
So I deficient am in every part.

Thou art all-wise, all-good, all-great, divine,
Yea, Thou art God: eternity is thine,
While I, a thing of clay,
The creature of a day,
Pass shadow-like, a breath, that comes and flees away.

What is my life, my strength, my righteousness,
That I should dare abide
Before thee, torn by passions numberless,
With soul unpurified!

III

My God, I know my sins are numberless,
More than I can recall to memory
Or tell their tale: yet some will I confess,
Even a few, though as a drop it be
    In all the sea.

I will declare my trespasses and sin
And peradventure silence then may fall

Upon their waves and billows' raging din,
And Thou wilt hear from heaven, when I call,
    And pardon all.

I have transgressed and sinned and turned aside
From Thy most holy precepts day by day,
I have rebelled, Thy law I have defied,
In scorn and folly, from the heavenward way
    Have gone astray.

Corrupted are my paths, and prone my heart
To deeds of evil. Righteous, O Most High,
In all that hast befallen me Thou art;
For just and faithful Thou hast been, but I
    Did wickedly.

IV

My God, if mine iniquity
Too great for all endurance be,
Yet for Thy name's sake pardon me.
For if in Thee I may not dare
To hope, who else will hear my prayer?
Therefore, although Thou slay me, yet
In Thee my faith and trust is set:

And though Thou seekest out my sin,
From Thee to Thee I fly to win
A place of refuge, and within
Thy shadow from Thy anger hide,
Until Thy wrath be turned aside.
Unto Thy mercy I will cling,
Until Thou hearken pitying :
Nor will I quit my hold of Thee
Until Thy blessing light on me.

Remember, O my God, I pray,
How Thou hast formed me out of clay,
What troubles set upon my way.
Do Thou not, then, my deeds requite
According to my sins aright,
But with Thy mercy infinite.
For well I know, through good and ill
That Thou in love has chastened still,
Afflicting me in faithfulness,
That Thou my latter end may'st bless.

v

Therefore, O Lord, let now Thy mercies be
Inclined towards me, and my sins forgot,
And let Thy wrath be turned away from me,
    So that I perish not.

Mayest Thou, O my God, to me return
With mercy, and in Thy beneficence,
Cause me to seek Thy face, the joy to learn
    Of perfect penitence.

Incline Thy ear to me my prayer to grant,
Prepare my heart Thy mercy to implore,
Teach me Thy law, and in my soul implant
    Thy fear for evermore.

O may it be Thy gracious will to guard
Me from all deeds of evil passions born,
From off my path the evil powers to ward,
    Temptation, sin, and scorn.

Be with my lips in prayer, and guard my way,
Lest with my tongue I sin. Save me from harm,
And give me refuge through life's stormy day
    Within Thy sheltering arm.

VI

My God, I know that those who plead
To Thee for grace and mercy need
All their good deeds should go before,
And wait for them at heaven's high door.
But no good deeds have I to bring,

No righteousness for offering,
No service for my Lord and King.

Yet hide not Thou Thy face from me,
Nor cast me out afar from Thee:
But when Thou bid'st my life to cease,
O may'st Thou lead me forth in peace
Unto the world to come, to dwell
Among Thy pious ones, who tell
Thy glories inexhaustible

There let my portion be with those
Who to eternal life arose,
There purify my heart aright
In Thy light to behold the light.
Raise me from deepest depths to share
Heaven's endless joys of praise and prayer,
That I may evermore declare:
Though Thou wast angered, Lord, I will give thanks to Thee,
For past is now thy wrath, and Thou dost comfort me.

VII

Lord, Thy heavenly love bestoweth
All the good my spirit knoweth,
All my life-long benedictions

From Thy gracious hand they came.
May Thy hallowed fear enfold me,
May Thy perfect law uphold me,
That my soul in glad submission
To Thy great and awful name,
Praise and prayer and thanks outpouring,
Sanctifying and adoring,
May exalt it, and extol it, and its unity proclaim.

Blessed, exalted, glorified,
Praised, extolled, and sanctified,
  Art Thou, O Lord,
  And eternally adored,
And Thy unity made known
By the righteous and the just,
By those risen from the dust,
By the angels round Thy throne,
And by those who ceaselessly
Do proclaim Thy unity.

For among the mighty none
Are like unto Thee, nor one
Of their works is like to Thine.
Thou by all the host divine
By cherubim and seraphim,
Radiant spirits manifold,
Unto Thee acceptable

Art in heaven above extolled.
And Thy people Israel
With awe and reverence proclaim :
"God is One and One His name!"

Thou art God in highest heaven,
On this earth, that Thou hast given
Unto man, and none beside Thee
Was, or is, or e'er shall be.
May my words of adoration,
May my inward meditation,
O my Rock and my Redeemer, prove acceptable to
    Thee.

THE HEART'S DESIRE

(Hymn for the Day of Atonement)

Lord ! unto Thee are ever manifest
My inmost heart's desires, though unexpress'd
In spoken words. Thy mercy I implore
Even for a moment—then to die were bless'd.

O ! if I might but win that grace divine,
Into Thy hand, O Lord, I would resign
My spirit then, and lay me down in peace
To my repose, and sweetest sleep were mine.

Afar from Thee in midst of life I die,
And life in death I find, when Thou art nigh.
Alas ! I know not how to seek Thy face,
Nor how to serve and worship Thee most High.

O lead me in Thy path, and turn again
My heart's captivity, and break in twain
The yoke of folly: teach me to afflict
My soul, the while I yet life's strength retain.

Despise not Thou my lowly penitence:
Ere comes the day, when deadened every sense,
My limbs too feeble grown to bear my weight,
A burden to myself, I journey hence.

When to the all-consuming moth a prey,
My wasted form sinks slowly to decay,
And I shall seek the place my fathers sought,
And find my rest there where at rest are they.

I am on earth a sojourner, a guest,
And my inheritance is in her breast,
My youth has sought as yet its own desires,
When will my soul's true welfare be my quest?

The world is too much with me, and its din
Prevents my search eternal peace to win.
How can I serve my Maker when my heart
Is passion's captive, is a slave to sin?

But should *I* strive to scale ambition's height,
Who with the worm may sleep ere fall of night?

Or can I joy in happiness to-day
Who know not what may chance by morning's light?

My days and nights will soon, with restless speed,
Consume life's remnant yet to me decreed :
Then half my body shall the winds disperse,
Half will return to dust, as dust indeed.

What more can I allege ? From youth to age
Passion pursues me still at every stage.
If Thou art not my portion, what is mine?
Lacking Thy favour, what my heritage?

Bare of good deeds, scorched by temptation's fire,
Yet to Thy mercy dares my soul aspire :
But wherefore speech prolong, since unto Thee,
O Lord, is manifest my heart's desire?

SERVANT OF GOD

(HYMN FOR THE DAY OF ATONEMENT)

O WOULD that I might be
A servant unto Thee,
Thou God, by all adored!
Then, though by friends out-cast,
Thy hand would hold me fast
And draw me near to Thee, my King and Lord!

Spirit and flesh are Thine,
O Heavenly Shepherd mine:
My hopes, my thoughts, my fears, thou seest all,
Thou measurest my path, my steps dost know.
When thou upholdest, who can make me fall?
When Thou restrainest, who can bid me go?
O would that I might be
A servant unto thee,
Thou God, by all adored!

Then, though by friends out-cast,
Thy hand would hold me fast,
And draw me near to Thee, my King and Lord!

Fain would my heart come nigh
To Thee, O God, on high,
But evil thoughts have led me far astray
From the pure path of righteous government.
Guide thou me back into Thy holy way,
And count me not as one impenitent.
O would that I might be
A servant unto Thee,
Thou God, by all adored!
Then, though by friends out-cast,
Thy hand would hold me fast,
And draw me near to Thee, my King and Lord!

If in my youth, I still
Fail to perform Thy will,
What can I hope when age shall chill my breast?
Heal me, O Lord; with Thee is healing found—
Cast me not off, by weight of years oppress'd,
Forsake me not when age my strength has bound.
O would that I might be
A servant unto Thee,
Thou God, by all adored!
Then, though by friends out-cast,

Thy hand would hold me fast,
And draw me near to Thee, my King and Lord!

Contrite and full of dread,
I mourn each moment fled
Midst idle follies roaming desolate:
I sink beneath transgressions manifold,
That from Thy presence keep me separate,
Nor can sin-darkened eyes Thy light behold.
O would that I might be
A servant unto Thee,
Thou God, by all adored!
Then though by friends out-cast,
Thy hand would hold me fast,
And draw me near to Thee, my King and Lord!

So lead me that I may
Thy sovereign will obey.
Make pure my heart to seek Thy truth divine,
When burns my wound, be Thou with healing near!
Answer me, Lord! for sore distress is mine,
And say unto Thy servant, I am here!
O would that I might be
A servant unto Thee,
Thou God, by all adored!
Then, though by friends out-cast,
Thy hand would hold me fast,
And draw me near to Thee, my King and Lord!

MERCY AND PARDON

(Hymn for the Day of Atonement)

Come, let us bow and bend the knee,
And seek with souls contrite—
And hearts uplifted, ceaselessly
God's mercy infinite.

All we like sheep have gone astray,
But He will hear us when we pray,
So that we yet may find to-day
    Mercy and pardon.
For though our sins are numberless,
And daily we His law transgress,
Yet hope inspires the prayerful song:
"Unto the Lord our God belong
    Mercy and pardon."

God's loving mercies far exceed
The measure of our sin :

Then let us seek them in our need,
Our shelter there to win.
For though the wrath of God be just,
Yet, bending humbly to the dust,
We still may gain, in loving trust,
 Mercy and pardon.

Come, we will hasten penitent
To pray to Him Omniscient,
To raise again the prayerful song:
"Unto the Lord our God belong
 Mercy and pardon."

Man cannot by his works alone
His load of guilt annul.
Let him with prayers besiege the throne
Of Heaven most merciful.
To those who seek Him earnestly,
In penitent humility,
The Lord our God will multiply
 Mercy and pardon.

O'er heaven above, o'er earth below,
His wide extended blessings flow,
Then raise with joy the prayerful song:
"Yea to the Lord our God belong
 Mercy and pardon."

WHILE YET WE DWELL ON EARTH

(Hymn for the Day of Atonement)

While yet we dwell on earth
God watches us, to whom His word gave birth,
And waits, in love and graciousness,
For penitence, that He our latter end may bless.

Can man be provéd righteous in the sight.
Of God, to whom all hidden thoughts are known?
Yea, if his soul repent before his light
Is quenched—and thus alone—
Can he gain pardon and for sin atone.

Even darkness hideth naught from God on high,
The evil deeds man holds invisible
Will at the end against him testify.
Therefore for him 'tis well,
Confessing them, guilt's shadow to dispel.

Behold, the heaven of heavens is not pure
In the eyes of God: how much less man, defiled
By shame and sin, whom guilty thoughts allure.
Let him, the oft-beguiled,
Then muse on this, ere earth reclaim her child.

His treasured gold will not, in death's dark hour.
Ransom his soul: but if through life he cling
To mercy and to righteousness, their power
Will his redemption bring,
And he shall see the glory of the King.

'Tis good for man the law's mild yoke to bear,
With love and awe its statutes to obey
For his oft-faltering steps it will prepare
The path of right alway,
And lead him through the grave to heavenly day.

Lord, in Thy hand as potter's clay are we:
Do Thou sustain us on life's troubled shore,
And fill our hearts with love and fear of Thee,
So that we may adore
Thy name, and sing Thy praises evermore.

While yet we dwell on earth
God watches us, to whom His word gave birth,
And waits in love and graciousness
For penitence, that He our latter end may bless.

PALMS AND MYRTLES

(Hymn for the First Day of Tabernacles)

Thy praise, O Lord, will I proclaim
In hymns unto Thy glorious name.
O Thou Redeemer, Lord and King,
Redemption to Thy faithful bring!
Before thine altar they rejoice
With branch of palm, and myrtle-stem,
To Thee they raise the prayerful voice—
Have mercy, save and prosper them.

May'st Thou in mercy manifold,
Dear unto Thee Thy people hold,
When at Thy gate they bend the knee,
And worship and acknowledge Thee.
Do Thou their heart's desire fulfil,
Rejoice with them in love this day,
Forgive their sins, and thoughts of ill,
And their transgressions cast away.

They overflow with prayer and praise
To Him, who knows the future days.
Have mercy Thou, and hear the prayer
Of those who palms and myrtles bear.
Thee day and night they sanctify
And in perpetual song adore,
Like to the heavenly host, they cry
"Blessed art Thou for evermore."

CREATOR OF THE UNIVERSE

(Hymn for the Last Day of Tabernacles)

Creator of the universe, in Thee
Is all my strength, is all my might,
    Thy favour unto me
My gladness is, my soul's delight.

Did not Thy loving-kindnesses abound
My toil were vain, of profit reft,
    Thy mercy folds me round,
Thy glory guides me right and left.

Open to me the portals of Thy grace,
That I may come and enter in,
    And let Thy hand efface
The heavy record of my sin.

O may Thy love be magnified alway,
Thy kindness marvellous withal!
    And grant my prayer this day,
This eighth day of our festival.

SABBATH HYMN

Come forth, my friend, the bride to meet,
Come, O my friend, the Sabbath greet!

"Observe ye" and "remember" still
The Sabbath—thus His holy will
God in one utterance did proclaim.
The Lord is One, and One His name
To His renown and praise and fame.
    Come forth, my friend, the bride to meet,
    Come, O my friend, the Sabbath greet!

Greet we the Sabbath at our door,
Well-spring of blessing evermore,
With everlasting gladness fraught,
Of old ordained, divinely taught,
Last in creation, first in thought.
    Come forth, my friend, the bride to meet,
    Come, O my friend, the Sabbath greet!

Arouse thyself, awake and shine,
For, lo! it comes, the light divine.
Give forth a song, for over thee
The glory of the Lord shall be
Revealed in beauty speedily.
    Come forth, my friend, the bride to meet,
    Come, O my friend, the Sabbath greet!

Crown of thy husband, come in peace,
Come, bidding toil and trouble cease.
With joy and cheerfulness abide
Among thy people true and tried,
Thy faithful people—come, O bride!
    Come forth, my friend, the bride to meet,
    Come, O my friend, the Sabbath greet!

HYMN FOR THE CONCLUSION OF THE SABBATH

May He who sets the holy and profane
Apart, blot out our sins before His sight,
And make our numbers as the sand again,
    And as the stars of night.

The day declineth like the palm-tree's shade,
I call on God, who leadeth me aright,
The morning cometh—thus the watchman said—
    Although it now be night.

Thy righteousness is like Mount Tabor vast;
O let my sins be wholly put to flight,
Be they as yesterday, for ever past,
    And as a watch at night.

The peaceful season of my prayers is o'er,
Would that again had rest my soul contrite,

HYMN FOR CONCLUSION OF SABBATH

Weary am I of groaning evermore,
   I melt in tears each night.

Hear Thou my voice: be it not vainly sped,
Open to me the gates of lofty height;
For with the evening dew is filled my head,
   My locks with drops of night.

O grant me Thy redemption, while I pray,
Be Thou entreated, Lord of power and might,
In twilight, in the evening of the day,
   Yea, in the gloom of night.

Save me, O Lord, my God, I call on Thee!
Make me to know the path of life aright,
From sore and wasting sickness snatch Thou me,
   Lead me from day to night.

We are like clay within Thy hand, O Lord,
Forgive us all our sins both grave and light,
And day shall unto day pour forth the word,
   And night declare to night.

May He who sets the holy and profane
Apart, blot out our sins before His sight,
And make our numbers as the sand again,
   And as the stars of night.

HYMNS OF UNITY FOR THE SEVEN DAYS OF THE WEEK.

I

ETERNAL King, the heavens and earth are thine,
Thine are the seas and every living thing.
Thy hand upholds creation's vast design,
    Eternal King!

The mighty waters with Thy glory ring,
Unnumbered lands to chant Thy praise combine,
And kings of earth to Thee their worship bring.

Thy people Israel for Thy love benign
Blesses Thy name and joys Thy praise to sing.
Thou art the God of truth, the one, divine,
    Eternal King.

II

I worship Thee for all Thy boundless store
Of righteousness and mercy shown to me,
And for Thy holy book of sacred lore
    I worship Thee.

To Thee alone our fathers bent the knee
And Thee alone do we this day adore,
Bearing our witness to Thy unity.

Thou art our God, Thy favour we implore,
Thou art our Shepherd and Thy flock are we,
Therefore I bless Thy name, and evermore
    I worship Thee.

III

I KNOW it well: Thou art all good, all wise.
Thou slayest, but Thy touch death's power can quail;
Thou woundest, but Thy hand the balm supplies:
    I know it well.

Nor sin, nor grief can in Thy presence dwell,
Slumber and sleep come not unto Thine eyes,
Great God, eternal and unchangeable!

The soul of all mankind before Thee lies,
Thou searchest all their hearts, their thoughts canst tell,
Thou hearest graciously their prayerful cries:
    I know it well.

IV

We will extol the Lord of lords, whose name
Is evermore and everywhere adored.
In songs and hymns our lips His praise shall frame:
    We will extol the Lord!

He is the hope of Israel, His word
A lamp unto our feet, a guiding flame
To those who trust in Him with full accord.

He is through countless ages still the same,
The shield of our salvation and our sword,
And generations, each to each, proclaim:
    We will extol the Lord!

V

Who shall narrate Thy wonders wrought of old?
The utterance of the lips Thou didst create,
But all Thy majesty and power untold
          Who shall narrate?

Thy ways on earth in song we celebrate,
Though none may Thy similitude behold,
Yet know we by Thy works that Thou art great.

Thousands of angels, by Thy word controll'd,
To do Thy bidding Thy commands await:
Yet of them all, Thy wonders manifold
          Who shall narrate?

VI

ALONE didst Thou, O Lord, the heavens' wide tent
Uprear and bid the earth beneath be shown!
Thy word the oceans in their boundaries pent
        Alone.

No aid or counsel hadst Thou save Thine own,
When Thou with lights didst hang the firmament
And call the hosts celestial round Thy throne.

Thy works, in universal cadence blent,
Give praise to Thee and make Thy glory known:
Thou madest all, great God beneficent,
        Alone!

VII

Of old Thou didst the Sabbath bless and praise,
Because thereon Thou didst Thy work behold,
Completed in the sun's new-kindled rays
   Of old.

Bless Thou this day with mercies manifold
Thy people, that in love and awe obeys
Thy word and chants Thy righteousness untold

Lord, we desire to do Thy will always!
Make pure our hearts like thrice refined gold,
And these, our prayers, accept as in the days
   Of old

GRACE AFTER MEALS

Our Rock, with loving care,
According to His word,
Bids all His bounty share;
Then let us bless the Lord.

His flock our Shepherd feeds
With graciousness divine,
He satisfies our needs
With gifts of bread and wine.
Therefore with one accord
We will His name adore,
Proclaiming evermore
None holy as the Lord.
                        Our Rock, etc.

The land desired so long,
Our father's heritage,
Inspires our prayer and song

To God from age to age:
His bounteous gifts afford
Our sustenance each day,
His mercy is our stay—
Yea, faithful in the Lord.
    Our Rock, etc.

O be Thy mercy moved,
Our Rock, to dwell with us,
With Zion, thy beloved,
Our temple glorious.
May we, redeemed, restored,
Be led there every one
By David's holy Son,
The anointed of the Lord.
    Our Rock, etc.

Thy city build once more,
Thy temple walls upraise,
There will we Thee adore
With joyful songs of praise,
Thee, merciful, adored,
We bless and sanctify,
With wine-cups filled up high,
By blessings of the Lord.
    Our Rock, etc.

GRACE FOR THE SABBATH

To Israel this day is joy ever bless'd,
Is light and is gladness, a Sabbath of rest.

Thou Sabbath of rest,
To a people distress'd,
To sorrowful souls,
A strong soul hast given.
From souls tempest-driven
Thou takest their sighing,
Thou takest their sighing,
Thou Sabbath of rest

This Sabbath of rest,
O God, thou hast bless'd
And hallowed above
All the days of creation,
The care-laden nation
To peace and hope wakens,
To peace and hope wakens,
This Sabbath of rest.

To slaves giveth rest
The Sabbath behest,
We are free while we keep
Its statutes appointed.
A gift well anointed
We bring thee, O loved One,
We bring thee, O loved One,
The Sabbath of rest.

O gladden our rest,
And our sanctuary bless'd
Restore thou, O Lord,
And grant Thy salvation
To Israel Thy nation,
Extolling and praising,
Extolling and praising
The Sabbath of rest.

To Israel this day is joy ever bless'd
Is light and is gladness, a Sabbath of rest.

MORNING PRAYER

My God, the soul Thou gavest me is pure,
    Created, formed by Thee,
    And breath'd into me.
Within the body's veil it will endure,
Until Thou call it hence
To live again through Thy beneficence
While I yet live, my lips shall still recall
That Thou art King and Lord,
Ruler of all, whose word
Creates and forms, sustains and governs all.
    Bless'd for evermore
Art Thou, who dost the dead to life restore.

EVENING PRAYER

Bless'd art Thou, O Lord of all,
Who mak'st the bands of sleep to fall
Upon mine eyes, and slumber press
Mine eyelids down with heaviness.

God of my fathers, may it be
Thy will, this night to suffer me
To lay me down in peace and rise
In peace, when morning gilds the skies.

From thoughts of ill my slumber keep,
And, lest the sleep of death I sleep,
O Lighten Thou mine eyes, for Thou
Lord, dost with light the eye endow.

Bless'd art Thou, O Lord most high,
Who in Thy glorious majesty,
And in Thy gracious love hast given
Light upon earth and light in heaven.

LORD OF THE UNIVERSE. (ADON OLAM)

Lord of the Universe, who reigned
Ere earth and heaven's fashioning,
When to create the world he deigned,
Then was His name proclaiméd King.

And at the end of days shall He
The dreaded one, still reign alone,
Who was, who is, and still will be
Unchanged upon His glorious throne.

And He is one, His powers transcend,
Supreme, unfathomed, depth and height,
Without beginning, without end,
His are dominion, power, and might.

My God and my Redeemer He,
My Rock in sorrow's darkest day,
A help and refuge unto me,
My cup's full portion, when I pray.

My soul into His hand divine
Do I commend : I will not fear,
My body with it I resign,
I dread no evil : God is near.

THE LIVING GOD WE PRAISE. (YIGDAL)

THE living God we praise, exalt, adore!
He was, He is, He will be evermore.

No unity like unto His can be,
Eternal, inconceivable is He.

No form or shape has th' incorporeal One,
Most holy beyond all comparison.

He was, ere aught was made in heaven or earth,
But His existence has no date or birth.

Lord of the Universe is He proclaimed,
Teaching His power to all His hand has framed.

He gave His gift of prophecy to those
In whom He gloried, whom He loved and chose.

No prophet ever yet has filled the place
Of Moses, who beheld God face to face.

Through Him (the faithful in His house) the Lord
The law of truth to Israel did accord.

This law God will not alter, will not change
For any other through time's utmost range.

He knows and heeds the sercet thoughts of man:
He saw the end of all ere aught began.

With love and grace doth He the righteous bless,
He metes out evil unto wickedness.

He at the last will His anointed send,
Those to redeem, who hope, and wait the end.

God will the dead to life again restore,
Praised be His glorious name for evermore.

www.ingramcontent.com/pod-product-compliance
Lightning Source LLC
Chambersburg PA
CBHW020911230426
43666CB00008B/1409